COCKTAILS

— THE NEW CLASSICS —

• 13-Digit ISBN: 978-1-64643-408-4 • 10-Digit ISBN: 1-64643-408-0 • This book may
be ordered by mail from the publisher. Please include $5.99 for postage and
handling. • Please support your local bookseller first! • Books published by
Cider Mill Press Book Publishers are available at special discounts
for bulk purchases in the United States by corporations, insti-
tutions, and other organizations. For more information,
please contact the publisher. • Cider Mill Press
Book Publishers • "Where good books are
ready for press" • 501 Nelson Place
• Nashville, Tennessee 37214
• cidermillpress.com •

Typography: Opti-
ma, Sofia Pro
• Image
Credits:
Pages
4 – 5 ,
6–7, 8–9,
10–11, 19,
2 0 – 2 1 ,
23, 26,
8 4 – 8 5 ,
109, 113,
140, 239,
258–259,
270–271,
2 9 1 ,
310–311,
322, 335,
363, and
389 used
u n d e r
official
l i c e n s e
f r o m
Shutter-
s t o c k .
c o m .
P a g e s
256–257 used
under Creative Commons
license. All other images courtesy of Cider Mill Press.
Printed in China • 23 24 25 26 27 DSC 6 5 4 3 2

COCKTAILS

— THE NEW CLASSICS —

CIDER MILL PRESS

BOOK PUBLISHERS

CONTENTS

INTRODUCTION

All of a sudden, you can find a clarified milk punch in a sleepy mountain town. In chain restaurants, which thrive by shooting for the dead center of the road, carefully constructed drinks featuring mezcal, amaro, and housemade herbal syrups are commonplace.

Today, no matter where you live, the expectation is that you can walk into any respectable restaurant and be presented with a cocktail list filled with thoughtful drinks centered around innovative bespoke ingredients and spirits pulled from the far-flung corners of the globe.

It is so commonplace that we take it for granted, barely raise an eyebrow.

But from the vantage point of 40 years ago, it is unthinkable, as unlikely as the powerful computers we now carry in our pockets.

What bridged the impossibly enormous gap between these two worlds?

The craft cocktail movement.

The term revolution has now been used to the point where it has lost some of its power to convey dramatic change, but its true meaning articulates the sea change that various bartenders and mixologists have ushered into the drinks world.

Back in bartending's dark days, otherwise known as the 1980s, most people's acquaintance with cocktails was a Rum & Coke, a Jack & Ginger or Seven & Seven, the messy mélange that is the Long Island Iced Tea, a Margarita, Daiquiri, or Tom Collins made from a prefabricated mix better suited to a car engine than a cocktail, or a finger or two of vodka slipped into some juice made from concentrate.

Cocktails tended to be imbalanced and overwhelmingly inclined toward sweetness, and were seen primarily as a quicker means of meeting a solitary end: intoxication.

Of course, any darkness always has a few points of light. In New York, Dale DeGroff was emphasizing the use of fresh ingredients and reinvigorating long-lost classics at the famed Rainbow Room. In London, Dick Braidsell was passing along the invaluable secrets of the craft to the younger generation and showing how a sense of play could pay dividends in the bartending world, creating drinks like the Bramble (see page 98) and the Espresso Martini that are now viewed as standards. And in Tokyo, Kazuo Uyeda was perfecting the techniques that have now stationed him as a mythological figure in the craft cocktail world.

From that inauspicious moment, the movement slowly gained steam, with fanatics honing in on every element from measuring—eyeballing the amounts, long held as a sign of expertise at top-level bars, was out; using a jigger to ensure the ratios in a drink were always the same, was in—to whether a bar spoon should start at the far end of the glass and "pull" a particular cocktail when stirring, or inserted in the near side and "push" the liquid.

Once the fundamentals had spread throughout the industry, the imaginations and passions of the particular individuals involved began to flourish. Phil Ward shaped his Pages 256–257 used under Creative Commons license. All for mezcal into the Oaxaca Old Fashioned, putting New York's Death & Co. on the map, and helping to transform mezcal from a curiosity that people knew only (and erronesously) "as the one with the worm" to a global sensation. Martin Cate helped to drag tiki back from the dead and ended up winning a James Beard Award. Nicolas Torres used his passion for the bountiful agriculture of California to transform the San Francisco scene. Ryan Chetiyawardana turned his focus on innovation, sustainability, and improved service to eschew previously thought to be fundamental components such as citrus and ice, opening up many possibilities for inventive bartenders in the future.

This book aims to capture each step of this movement, and help others see where it is pointing. It seeks not only to celebrate the new classics that have been created, but to instruct, illuminate the attention to detail, imagination, and craft that have gone into them. It desires to do exactly what those bartenders whose contributions are collected here wanted—get someone to take a step back and appreciate the moment, to entertain while also exposing their customers to something new, something different, to express a passion, to perfect a craft.

BAR SPOON

JIGGER

HAWTHORNE
STRAINER

MUDDLER

ICE TONGS

COBBLER
SHAKER

MEASURING
SPOON

ZESTER /
LEMON ZESTER

TOOLS
OF
THE
TRADE

One of the nice things about getting into modern mixology is that you don't need to purchase all that many things in order to start mixing cocktails. Still, there are some rudimentary supplies that are necessary if you want to try your hand at this game.

The following pages contain the must-haves for a basic home bar. Keep in mind that you don't have to break the bank to get started, but between glassware and bar tools, a little money will need to be spent. You can find basic bar and glassware sets on specialty sites like Cocktail Kingdom, as well as other online retailers. As with anything, the options will fit lots of budgets. If you are tight on funds, don't be deterred by used items. Soap and water come pretty cheap and you might find some real bargains on vintage gear to boot. Same goes for antique shops and yard sales. Hell, your parents might have some of the tools you need stashed away in a closet or basement. Nothing wrong with a little scavenging for a good cause.

ESSENTIALS

Jigger: A jigger is just a fancy name for the most common measuring tool in a bartender's arsenal, allowing you to quickly and easily measure ounces or parts. Most jiggers have a similar shape and capacity to a shot glass (about 1 to 1½ ounces).

Mixing glass: This is nothing more than a tall glass in which to stir a drink. Typically, a pint glass is used, but in a pinch, you can use any glass large enough to hold the necessary ingredients and a few ice cubes. You can also splurge for a higher-end mixing glass that will have a spout to make pouring easier.

Cocktail shaker: A cocktail shaker provides a simple way to mix a cocktail, both combining the necessary ingredients, chilling them with ice, and diluting the cocktail slightly, which removes any bite from the included spirits and allows their flavors to come to the fore. A basic cocktail shaker is relatively inexpensive, and you are better off purchasing this specific tool than trying to jury-rig a shaker for yourself.

two-piece shakers, consisting of two conical containers with flat bottoms, with one of the cones larger than the other. Known as a "Boston" or "French" shaker, these tend to be favored by professional bartenders because their "throw," the amount of space inside for the ingredients and ice to be combined, is greater than in the squatter Cobbler shaker. For more on the advantages and disadvantages of each, turn to page 18.

Strainers: Used in tandem with either a mixing glass or a Boston shaker, the Hawthorne strainer simply strains the cocktail after it has been mixed. The strainer's spring keeps the ice cubes (in the case of a mixing glass) or cubes and ice chips (in the case of a Boston shaker) out of a drink. Because the ice used to mix a cocktail has already started to melt, the strainer is an important tool for keeping a cocktail from becoming overly watered down.

You may also come across a Julep strainer as you start making your way into the world of mixology. This strainer, which was the predecessor to the Hawthorne, is a perforated, concave disk. It has fallen out of common use, but some bartenders prefer it when straining a cocktail containing small pieces of herb or a large amount of pulp.

A small, fine-mesh strainer is also a good tool to have, as you will need to use it along with one of the previously mentioned strainers when a particular recipe directs you to double strain the cocktail into the glass.

Paring knife: Chances are, there's already one in your kitchen, and it is essential for crafting the lemon twists, lime wheels, and other garnishes that are a crucial part of a number of cocktails.

Muddler: Similar to a pestle, this simple tool is used to mash ("muddle") ingredients such as fruits or herbs. Muddling fruits releases the juice within, adding a fresh characteristic to a drink, while muddling certain herbs will help activate their flavors. A simple muddler can often be found on the top end of a Cobbler shaker, though more refined muddlers are available for minimal cost.

bar spoon. There are numerous styles of bar spoons, but most take the form of a spoon with a small bowl and a long, spiral shaft. Used in conjunction with a mixing glass, the purpose of the bar spoon is to quickly and easily stir any cocktail. You can use any spoon—you just may find it more difficult to navigate the ice cubes. You will also come across some recipes that call for a "bar spoon" of a certain ingredient, which is equivalent to 1 teaspoon.

Swizzle stick: A small stick used to quickly chill and aerate drinks, most commonly used in cocktails that feature crushed ice. Again, there's no need to break the bank when purchasing a swizzle stick, but it can be a valuable addition to a mixologist's kit.

Blender: Essential for frozen drinks, a blender is also very handy for turning fruit into a puree that can add a velvety texture to a cocktail.

NEXT LEVEL

None of the following items are required to make great cocktails, but, as you'll see in a few of the recipes, the quest to push the boundaries of what mixology can be and what ingredients incorporated has ushered some new implements into the bar.

Immersion blender: As mixologists around the globe's continue to push the boundaries in terms of the ingredients they include in their cocktails, and become increasingly influenced by what's going on in some of the world's best kitchens, the immersion blender, with its versatility and speed, has become a reliable tool in the execution of avant-garde cocktails.

Sous-Vide machine: The world's best bars have embraced this widespread culinary revolution, using its precision to create reliable and repeatable infusions. While far from necessary, a sous-vide machine will open up a world of possibilities to the ambitious and inventive mixologist.

Rotary evaporator: Those with a science background will recognize this from the lab, but some bartenders have begun to use these high-tech extractors to create small batches of bespoke spirits that result in cocktails that can't be found anywhere else.

GLASSWARE

Cocktail glasses: The elegant promise of its thin stem and triangular bowl has become inseparable from the very idea of a cocktail, as evidenced by the name and its frequent inclusion on a bar's signage. It is typically utilized in cocktails that are served "up," such as the Martini.

Collins & highball glasses: Tall and skinny and basically interchangeable, though Collins glasses are taller. Most commonly used in drinks that contain ice and a carbonated element such as club soda.

Rocks glasses: Also known as Old Fashioned glasses, these are meant for cocktails that are served "neat" and on the rocks. They are between 8 and 10 ounces; double Old Fashioned glasses are typically only a couple ounces larger and used for cocktails served over ice.

Coupe: The coupe has started to replace the traditional cocktail glass as the go-to for drinks that are served up, as its sleek curves lend an appealing refinement to a drink.

Shot glasses: There is no standard size for a shot glass, but most land between 1¼ and 1½ ounces. They can be used to measure parts for a cocktail or to serve alcohol, both straight up and mixed.

Champagne flutes & wineglasses: The thin bowl and delicate stem of a Champagne flute is a must for any sparkling cocktail, while a wineglass adds a note of sophistication to the proceedings when used to **hold a cocktail.**

ICE

Everyone is familiar with ice as a substance. It cools down a drink and it makes the roads a nightmare in the winter. When it comes to cocktails, there are a few things you need to know. Ice is one of the most important elements in a cocktail. It helps enhance the presentation, as few sights are more eye-catching than a frosted glass filled with clear, gleaming cubes and spheres, and it is an invaluable tool—either to cool down your drink as it is being shaken or stirred, or adding a little water to your creation in order to soften some of the harsher elements. Just as low-quality spirits can spell doom for a drink, bad ice can also sink a cocktail. Considering this, it's no surprise that some high-end bars have expensive machines to make blocks of clear, perfect ice; if you go on YouTube and look up Japanese bartenders and ice, you will see individuals wire-cutting a chunk of ice from an almost transparent block and then chipping away until they have a Platonic sphere that fits perfectly into a glass.

I'm going to make an assumption that most people reading this don't own a bar, aren't going to spend thousands of dollars on a machine that makes perfect ice, and don't have the time to hand-carve ice for each drink. But that doesn't mean you can't procure first-rate ice at home.

First off, use the best water you can get your hands on. The better the water, the better the ice—pretty straightforward. Filtering what comes out of your tap is a must. Spring or distilled water are definitely worth considering. If crystal-clear ice is of the utmost importance, you'll want to use distilled water, boil it twice, and let it cool completely before adding it to the ice-cube trays. Distilling the water removes most of the air and minerals from it, which are the elements that create cloudy ice. Boiling it will extract whatever air and minerals remain, and the care taken with the resulting cubes will be transparent to all.

Once you've sorted out the water, you need something that can provide the desired form. Standard plastic ice-cube trays can work in a pinch, but you may want to make a small investment in some silicone trays that produce larger cubes and spheres. The increased surface area will cause the ice to melt slower, helping you avoid the dreaded "watery drink" phenomenon.

Another thing to remember: ice trays take on the smells of the freezer (though metal trays do not hold onto odors as dearly as plastic and silicone trays). Since no one wants ice that smells like a batch of stew, we suggest the following:

Wash your ice trays before a big party—soap and water should be fine with regular trays; soap, water, and baking soda is the move with silicone trays because even though they make amazing ice, the silicone picks up more odors than a standard tray. In fact, giving the freezer a good scrub before making ice for the big party wouldn't hurt.

Have a set of trays that is only used for cocktail ice—ice trays can't pick up freezer smells if they aren't in the freezer all of the time. Keep this set in resealable plastic bags in a kitchen cabinet (though be sure to keep them away from the oven and stove since cooking will impart odors as well) to reduce the aromas your ice cubes pick up.

Make fresh ice for each party—the best way to avoid stinky, stale ice is to minimize the time the ice is in the freezer, meaning you'd be wise to make fresh batches the day of or the day before the party.

If you need to make crushed ice, don't rely on the refrigerator dispenser. Rather, get a Lewis bag and mallet. Back in the 19th century, these canvas sacks were a staple in bars. Just add some of your freshly made cubes to the bag, give it a couple of whacks, and, voila, you have homemade crushed ice that is perfect for cocktails, as well as a nice stress reliever.

MIXING COCKTAILS

Where the rubber meets the road. It's nice to have outfitted yourself with all of the required kit and maintained a fanatical devotion to high-quality ingredients, but if you don't know how to utilize them properly, all that careful preparation and passion ends up not mattering much.

Luckily, there aren't too many moving parts when it comes to mixing cocktails. Consistently excellent results are accessible if one adheres to a few fundamentals.

To start, always add the ingredients to the cocktail shaker or mixing glass before adding the ice.

When you do add ice, the more, the merrier. If you don't use enough ice, it will melt in the mixing vessel and you'll be left with a drink that is too watery for anyone's liking. A good rule of thumb is to fill the cocktail shaker or mixing glass about two-thirds of the way with ice. It's also imperative that you use full-sized cubes instead of crushed ice to avoid overdiluting the cocktail. Another good thing to keep in mind: the larger the surface area of the ice cubes, the longer you will have to shake or stir the cocktail to properly chill, combine, and dilute it.

As for whether to use a cocktail shaker or a mixing glass to combine the cocktail, you want to take the ingredients and the cocktail's desired effect into account. Drinks containing juice, dairy, or egg white should be shaken, as the additional force will aerate the cocktail and create a thick, velvety froth that is as pleasing to the eye as it is to the tongue.

Drinks that are comprised only of spirits (unless one of them is a cream liqueur) should be stirred, since you are not after froth, but a smooth and strong consistency featuring minimal dilution. Some believe that shaking a cocktail which does not have an aerating element to cushion it will "bruise" the liquor, lending it a bitterness that is sure to stand out amid the delicate play of flavors in a mixed drink.

Cocktails that contain a carbonated element such as club soda should be stirred, since shaking it will remove all of the carbonation. This is such a concern that it is recommended you add the fizzy component to the cocktail after it has been strained into the glass, and then stir gently so as to just integrate it with the other ingredients.

Now, as some probably wondered upon encountering the "stir spirits-only cocktails" maxim, to the age-old debate that the fictional James Bond ignited when he insisted that his Martini be "shaken, not stirred."

The argument has been granted such weight that even scientists have entered the fray, conducting studies, performing research, and identifying empirical, quantifiable differences between the shaken and stirred Martini.

John Hayes, a food science professor at Penn State University, once told NPR that shaking a Martini dilutes the drink, giving it a more watery character. Unlike stirring, shaking a cocktail chips away at the ice, resulting in tiny flakes that melt as the drink warms. On the other hand, these tiny ice flakes help keep the drink cold for a longer period of time.

Bartender Darcy O'Neil, operating on the popular theory that Bond's preference was attributable to shaking being a better option for incorporating the oily quality of a potato vodka, performed tests which confirm that shaking a Martini made with potato vodka successfully dissipates that oil. He also agrees that shaking a Martini will make it colder, but notes that after 20 shakes or so, a cocktail has generally gotten as cold as it's going to get.

Culinary scientist Dave Arnold agrees with O'Neil that shaking a cocktail will make it colder, but points out that the ability to detect certain flavors is impeded when a drink becomes too cold. Sweetness, in particular, becomes more difficult to taste, and Arnold recommends adding a dash of Simple Syrup (see page 26) if you plan to shake a traditionally stirred cocktail.

So, what's the verdict?

Those in search of a traditional experience should stir a spirits-only drink such as the Martini. Those who want to ensure that the ingredients are combined as thoroughly as possible should try shaking their drink. Those looking for a colder drink should shake it. Those who desire a sweeter drink should stir it. In the end, the two methods produce different results, but which version is "better" is ultimately determined by personal preference.

While stirring will produce a cocktail that is less cold than one made by shaking, you still want the cocktail to be cold. This will take much longer with a mixing glass than with a shaker, around two to three times as long. To do this, add the ingredients to the mixing glass, fill it two-thirds of the way with ice, and then, working in a circular motion rather than up and down, use a bar spoon to stir the drink.

When it comes to shaking, it is up to you whether you want a Boston shaker or a Cobbler shaker to be your primary implement. Both have their advantages and disadvantages. The Boston shaker grants the ingredients and ice more space to be mixed in and allows them to emulsify better. The Cobbler shaker is easier to use, and some bartenders believe it makes it easier to control the ice in the shaker, keeping it away from the bottom and preventing too many small ice chips from entering a drink and eventually diluting it.

If using a Boston shaker, place the ingredients in the smaller container, fill the larger container two-thirds of the way with ice, quickly invert it over the container with the ingredients, taking care not to spill any ice, and then create a seal between the two containers. Hold each container with one hand and shake vigorously for about 12 seconds to properly chill and combine the ingredients. Gently tap the seal while holding onto the larger container in order to uncouple the pieces, place a Hawthorne strainer over the top of the container holding the drink, and strain the cocktail into the selected glass.

If using a Cobbler shaker, add the ingredients and fill it two-thirds of the way with ice. Secure the top and the cap and then shake vigorously for 15 seconds. The slightly longer shaking time is necessary due to the reduced volume of the Cobbler shaker. After 15 seconds, remove the cap and hold the shaker by the top as you strain the drink into the glass.

These techniques will suit almost every cocktail, but there are a few specialized methods which are called for in the recipes that follow, such as the Cuban roll and the swizzle method. When one of these are called for, a description of the method will be provided in the recipe.

GIN

Gin is not meant to "go gentle into that good night." If gin is in a cocktail, you'll know it. It's not necessarily the most difficult ingredient to work with (whiskey is harder); but its bold flavor just doesn't allow it to slink into the shadows the way other spirits can. Not to say that gin can't share the spotlight.

Today, many gins start with a neutral (flavorless) spirit and add botanicals afterward. Other producers elect to infuse their gin with essential oils, a method that allows for more affordable production, but is generally viewed as being less refined. Although the primary flavoring agent in gin will always be juniper, other botanicals such as coriander, angelica, grains of paradise, cassia, orris root, caraway, and elderflower are commonly used in the production of gin. And once Hendrick's, now one of the leading brands on the market, came out with a gin infused with cucumber and rose, the world of gin became far more wide open. These unorthodox additions tempered the juniper just enough that the other flavors were able to enter the picture, and the overwhelming response Hendrick's received alerted other producers that gin may be far more malleable than previously believed. This realization has resulted in a full-fledged "Gin Renaissance," which has given rise to gins made from uncommon bases such as apple brandy and malt, and others that employ noncanonical botanicals such as mugwort and sarsaparilla.

Despite the excitement these innovative takes have produced, the most popular style of gin remains London dry, which refers to a gin that starts with a completely neutral base spirit before flavoring agents are added. In keeping with its name, a London dry gin will typically be less sweet than other varieties, as well as higher in alcohol content. London dry is also known for the inclusion of citrus peel among its botanicals, an element often detectable in its aroma.

Another good thing to keep in mind: gin is the spirit that has probably benefitted the most from the craft distilling boom. Whether it be inventive flavoring options like spruce tips and chile peppers or barrel aging, these days most folks don't have to try too hard to find a great local gin that tastes better than the big-name options. As you'll see this explosion of artisan gins has gotten the mixology world excited, as the world's best bartenders have strained themselves to expose people to the surfeit of quality offerings currently on the market.

When working with gin to make a cocktail, try to use its powerful, herbal, and woodsy nature to your advantage. You don't want to try and hide it, as it will take too much effort, and likely leave you with a drink that tastes clumsy, inarticulate. Instead, you want to highlight its character as best you can, either surrounding it with floral, herbal, and vegetal elements, setting it off with fruity and spicy elements, or leaning upon gin's most reliable partners—citrus, vermouth, and bitters. Gin's strong flavor forces you to keep an important rule in cocktail making front of mind—it is always best to err on the side of simplicity with your creations. You'll see some exceptions to that approach here, as the leaders of the craft cocktail movement live to break such rules. But you will not see any cocktails where gin's strong backbone is saddled with too much to carry.

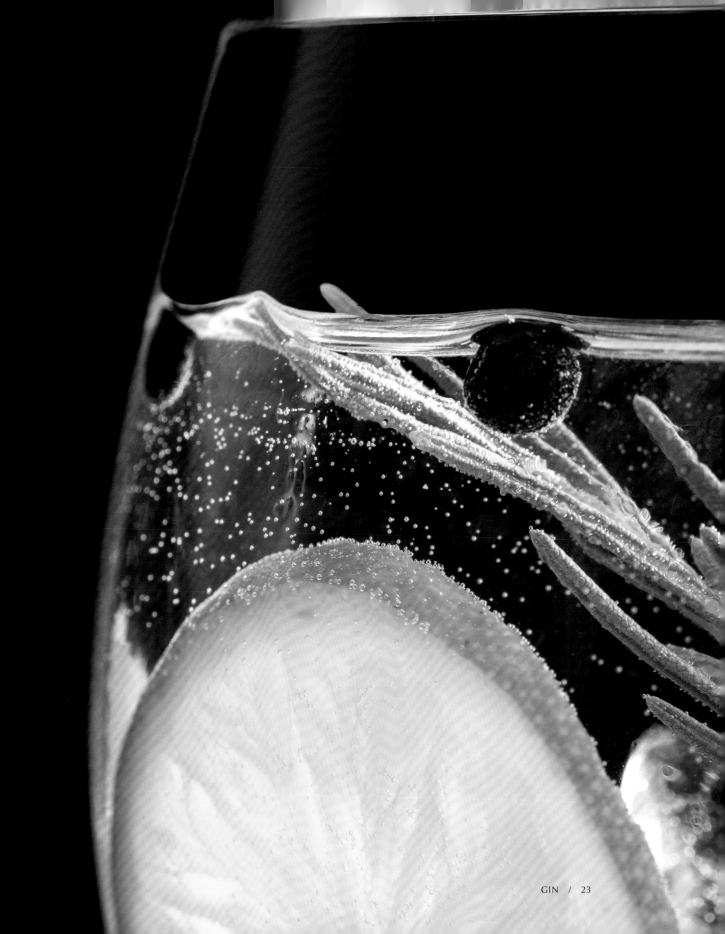

COOL LAGOON

An elegant drink from the mind of Samuel Kwok, the former bar manager at Hong Kong's lauded Quinary. At Quinary, Kwok sought to create drinks that would awaken all five senses, and became so good at it that the publication *Drinks International* once said the bar "might as well be working on the sixth [sense]."

---

6 fresh Thai basil leaves

Handful of fresh Italian basil leaves

1 oz. Pickled Jalapeño Pepper Syrup (see recipe)

1½ oz. Iron Balls gin

1 oz. Italicus rosolio di bergamotto liqueur

⅓ oz. Pavan Muscat liqueur

Dash of The Bitter Truth cucumber bitters

---

1. Place the basils in a cocktail shaker and muddle.

2. Add ice and the remaining ingredients and shake vigorously until chilled.

3. Strain over ice into the rocks glass filled with ice, garnish with the frozen grapes and fresh basil, and enjoy.

PICKLED JALAPEÑO PEPPER SYRUP: Place 1 cup sugar and 1 cup water in a saucepan and bring it to a boil, stirring to dissolve the sugar. Stir in 5 slices of pickled jalapeño and a dash of the brine, cook for 1 minute, and remove the pan from heat. Let the syrup cool completely and strain before using or storing.

GLASSWARE: Tiki mug

GARNISH: Dehydrated lemon wheel, fresh mint, dried chile pepper, freshly grated allspice

THE LAST BASTARD

The satisfying conclusion of the epic saga started by the Suffering Bastard cocktail.

⅔ oz. gin

⅔ oz. umeshu

⅔ oz. Bigallet China-China Amer liqueur

⅔ oz. fresh orange juice

2 bar spoons fresh lime juice

2 dashes of Dale DeGroff's pimento aromatic bitters

---

1. Place all of the ingredients, except for the bitters, in the tiki mug.

2. Insert a swizzle stick into the mixture and fill the glass halfway with crushed ice.

3. Use the swizzle method to mix the cocktail: place a swizzle stick between your hands, lower the swizzle stick into the drink, and quickly rub your palms together to rotate the stick as you move it up and down in the drink. When frost begins to form on the outside of the tiki mug, the drink is ready.

4. Top the glass with more crushed ice and the bitters, garnish with the dehydrated lemon wheel, fresh mint, dried chile pepper, and allspice, and enjoy.

GLASSWARE: Rocks glass

GARNISH: Fresh basil

GIN BASIL SMASH

Originally named the Gin Pesto, this refreshing, aromatic wonder swept around the globe shortly after Jörg Meyer created it at Paris' Le Lion in 2008.

---

12 fresh basil leaves

2 oz. gin

¾ oz. fresh lime juice

⅓ oz. Simple Syrup (see recipe)

---

1. Place the basil leaves in a cocktail shaker and muddle.

2. Add the remaining ingredients, fill the shaker two-thirds of the way with ice, and shake vigorously until chilled.

3. Double strain over ice into the rocks glass, garnish with the fresh basil, and enjoy.

SIMPLE SYRUP: Place 1 cup sugar and 1 cup water in a saucepan and bring it to a boil, stirring to dissolve the sugar. Remove the pan from heat and let the syrup cool completely before using or storing.

GARNISH: Lemon wheels, lime wheels, sprigs of fresh rosemary, sprigs of fresh thyme, manzanilla olive, dried juniper berries

GIN & TONIC

An excellent example of how the right garnishes can transform a classic cocktail.

---

2 oz. gin

Fever-Tree Mediterranean tonic, to taste

---

1. Pour the gin over ice into the wineglass.

2. Add tonic to taste, garnish with the lemon wheels, lime wheels, fresh rosemary, fresh thyme, manzanilla olive, and dried juniper berries, and enjoy.

GLASSWARE: Coupe

GARNISH: Sprigs of fresh thyme

CALIFORNIA COOLER

For the cordial, choose a reasonably priced Sauvignon Blanc that is dry with tropical and Muscat notes.

1½ oz. gin

¾ oz. freshly pressed celery juice

½ oz. Sauvignon Blanc & Thyme Cordial (see recipe)

½ oz. fresh lime juice

1 oz. Champagne

---

1. Place all of the ingredients, except for the Champagne, in a cocktail shaker, fill it two-thirds of the way with ice, and shake vigorously until chilled.

2. Double strain into the coupe and top with the Champagne.

3. Garnish with the fresh thyme and enjoy.

SAUVIGNON BLANC & THYME CORDIAL: Place a 750 ml bottle of Sauvignon Blanc in a saucepan and bring it to a gentle boil. Reduce the heat and simmer the wine for 10 minutes. Add ½ bunch of fresh thyme and a small chunk of fresh horseradish, peeled and lightly crushed, reduce the heat to low, and cook for 10 minutes. Add 4 cups sugar and stir until it has dissolved. Remove the pan from heat and let it cool completely. Strain before using or storing.

GLASSWARE: Collins glass

GARNISH: Peychaud's bitters, freshly grated nutmeg, fresh mint, grapefruit twist

ASYLUM HARBOR

An inventive concoction from one of tiki's modern masters, Martin Cate.

1¼ oz. Damrak gin

½ oz. Benedictine

¼ oz. almond liqueur

1 bar spoon St. Elizabeth allspice dram

½ oz. Ginger Syrup (see recipe)

½ oz. passion fruit puree

½ oz. fresh lime juice

¾ oz. grapefruit juice

---

1. Place all of the ingredients in a cocktail shaker, fill it two-thirds of the way with ice, and shake vigorously until chilled.

2. Strain over ice into the Collins glass, garnish with the bitters, nutmeg, fresh mint, and grapefruit twist, and enjoy.

GINGER SYRUP: Place 1 cup water and 1 cup sugar in a saucepan and bring the mixture to a boil, stirring to dissolve the sugar. Add a peeled 1-inch piece of fresh ginger, remove the pan from heat, and let the syrup cool completely. Strain before using or storing.

MARTIN CATE

It's hard to imagine the contemporary cocktail scene without Martin Cate. In the decade-plus since Cate unveiled Smuggler's Cove in San Francisco, it has in many ways become the most prominent rum-centric cocktail bar in the country and possibly in the whole world. It fits the perfect balance of island paradise/tiki atmosphere without the kitsch, mixed with a fanatical reverence for rum's many dimensions and deep history. Smuggler's Cove, simply put, is Cate's great thesis about rum. Then in 2015, Cate's scholarly slant toward rum set the stage for a deep-dive focus on gin at Whitechapel near San Francisco's City Hall, which he opened with partners Alex Smith and John Park. Beyond the bars, Cate is a James Beard Award–winning author, and a grand ambassador for the world of rum—in many ways, one of the first true celebrity bartenders of the 21st century.

VITAMIN SEA

A perfect cocktail to accompany oysters on the half-shell, carrying the freshness of a whitecap's foam.

1¼ oz. Hendrick's gin

¾ oz. Italicus rosolio di bergamotto liqueur

1 teaspoon Luxardo maraschino liqueur

⅞ oz. bergamot juice

½ oz. Lavender Syrup (see recipe)

Dash of ginger bitters

1 slice of fresh ginger

---

1. Place all of the ingredients in a cocktail shaker, fill it two-thirds of the way with ice, and shake vigorously until chilled.

2. Double strain into the coupe, spoon the Jasmine Air on top of the drink, and enjoy.

LAVENDER SYRUP: Place 1½ cups sugar, 1 cup water, and a generous handful of lavender in a saucepan and warm over medium heat, stirring to dissolve the sugar. Remove the pan from heat and let the syrup cool completely. Strain before using or storing.

JASMINE AIR: Place 9 oz. strongly brewed and chilled jasmine tea and ½ teaspoon soy lecithin in a container and stir to incorporate. Strain the mixture into a large bowl and work it with an immersion blender, trying to get as much air into the mixture as possible. Once the mixture is very foamy, use immediately.

GLASSWARE: Coupe

GARNISH: Rock samphire

THE ESCAPE

Mastiha liqueur, which can only be produced on the Greek island of Chios, adds robust herbal aromas to this cocktail.

---

3 dashes of ouzo, to rinse

2 oz. Beefeater London dry gin

½ oz. mastiha liqueur

¾ oz. dry vermouth

---

1. Rinse the coupe with the ouzo, discard it, and then chill the coupe in the freezer.

2. Place the remaining ingredients in a mixing glass, fill it two-thirds of the way with ice, and stir until chilled.

3. Strain into the chilled coupe, garnish with the rock samphire, and enjoy.

RINSE AND REPEAT

The technique utilized with the ouzo in The Escape is known as "rinsing," and it is a great way to add another accent to a cocktail. Rinsing a glass with Cognac, a liqueur, or a smoky, single-malt Scotch is a very simple and effective means of dressing up whiskey-based cocktails, and various liqueurs can be used to put a twist on drinks featuring any spirit. Misting the inside of the glass with various spirits or tinctures is another way to add a subtle hint. To do this, simply fill a spray bottle with your desired accent, strain the cocktail into the glass, and generously mist the glass above the liquid.

GLASSWARE: Rocks glass

GARNISH: Cucumber slice

CAPTAIN AWESOME

With almonds, apricot, and coconut winding through it, Mahiki makes for a tiki sensation.

---

2 cucumber slices

1 oz. London dry gin

1 oz. fresh lemon juice

½ oz. Ancho Reyes

½ oz. Mahiki coconut rum liqueur

½ oz. Demerara Syrup (see recipe)

1 oz. pineapple juice

---

1. Place the cucumber slices in a cocktail shaker and muddle.

2. Add the remaining ingredients, fill the shaker two-thirds of the way with ice, and shake vigorously until chilled.

3. Strain over a large ice cube into the rocks glass, garnish with the slice of cucumber, and enjoy.

DEMERARA SYRUP: Place 1 cup water in a saucepan and bring it to a boil. Add ½ cup demerara sugar and 1½ cups sugar and stir until they have dissolved. Remove the pan from heat and let the syrup cool completely before using or storing.

GLASSWARE: Double rocks glass

GARNISH: Slice of kiwi and sprigs of rosemary

PANDA LATINO

Herbal, sour, and ever-so-slightly salty, this cocktail is the perfect lead-in to a multi-course dinner party out on the patio in summer.

⅔ oz. gin

1 kiwi fruit, peeled

1⅓ oz. Herb Tea (see recipe)

⅔ oz. St-Germain

2 bar spoons fresh lemon juice

⅓ teaspoon freshly grated Parmesan cheese

---

1. Place all of the ingredients in a mason jar and use an immersion blender to emulsify the mixture.

2. Fill the double rocks glass with crushed ice and pour the cocktail over it.

3. Top the drink with more crushed ice, garnish with the kiwi and rosemary, and enjoy.

HERB TEA: Place fresh rosemary, fresh thyme, fresh oregano, and black peppercorns in a cup, pour hot water over the top, and steep overnight. The precise herb ratio isn't important, but the strength of the tea is, which is the reason for the lengthy steeping time. Strain before using or storing.

2 bar spoons fresh lime juice

3 drops of orange-flavored olive oil

1 bar spoon lime zest

---

1. Place all of the ingredients in a container and use an immersion blender to puree the mixture.

2. Add the puree to a cocktail shaker, fill it two-thirds of the way with ice, and shake vigorously until chilled.

3. Strain into the goblet and enjoy.

FENNEL SYRUP: Place 3½ oz. Simple Syrup (see page 26) and 2 tablespoons fennel seeds in a blender and pulse to combine. Strain before using or storing.

KAIKAN FIZZ

With all of the craft gins out there, you might be wondering what Gordon's is doing in a high-level cocktail. In truth, it's a standby for some of the world's best bartenders.

1⅓ oz. Gordon's London dry gin

½ oz. fresh lemon juice

1 bar spoon Simple Syrup (see page 26)

1 oz. milk

Club soda, to top

---

1. Place all of the ingredients, except for the club soda, in a cocktail shaker, fill it two-thirds of the way with ice, and shake vigorously until chilled.

2. Strain over ice into the Collins, top with club soda, stirring the drink vigorously with a bar spoon as you pour, and enjoy.

SHISUI

A cocktail as refreshing as a stroll through the mornin
in early May.

¾ oz. Suntory roku gin

½ oz. Mistia Muscat liqueur

2 bar spoons fresh lemon juice

1 bar spoon Ginger Syrup (see page 30)

1 bar spoon matcha liqueur

---

1. Place all of the ingredients in a cocktail shaker, fill i
   two-thirds of the way with ice, and shake vigorousl
   until chilled.

2. Strain into the cocktail glass and enjoy.

GLASSWARE: Cordial glass

GARNISH: Dried cabbage, gorgonzola cheese, honey

STRAWBERRY LETTER 23

A beautiful choice for a summer brunch, as everything from the juice to the choice of gin is designed to make the strawberry flavor pop.

---

1 oz. Koval gin

3 strawberries

2 bar spoons fresh lime juice

2 bar spoons freshly pressed cabbage juice

3 drops of Cinnamon-Infused White Wine Vinegar (see recipe)

3 drops of extra-virgin olive oil

Pinch of kosher salt

---

1. Place all of the ingredients in a container and use an immersion blender to emulsify the mixture.

2. Pour the mixture into a cocktail shaker, fill it two-thirds of the way with ice, and shake vigorously until chilled.

3. Strain into the cordial glass, garnish with the dried cabbage, gorgonzola cheese, and honey, and enjoy.

CINNAMON-INFUSED WHITE WINE VINEGAR: Place 2 cinnamon sticks and 7 oz. white wine vinegar in a mason jar and store in a cool, dark place for 1 week. Strain before using or storing.

SHERLOCK

A serve that showcases maraschino liqueur's talent to bind disparate flavors together.

---

1 oz. No.3 London dry gin

½ oz. Mistia Muscat liqueur

2 bar spoons Monin green banana syrup

2 bar spoons fresh lime juice

1 bar spoon Luxardo maraschino liqueur

---

1. Place all of the ingredients in a cocktail shaker, fill it two-thirds of the way with ice, and shake vigorously until chilled.

2. Strain into the cocktail glass and enjoy.

JFK

The late president's preference for Tanqueray gin is honored in this cocktail.

1½ oz. Tanqueray No. Ten gin

2 bar spoons Grand Marnier

2 bar spoons fino sherry

2 dashes of orange bitters

1 strip of orange peel

---

1. Place all of the ingredients, except for the orange peel, in a mixing glass, fill it two-thirds of the way with ice, and stir until chilled.

2. Strain into the cocktail glass. Hold the strip of orange peel about 2 inches above a lit match for a couple of seconds. Twist and squeeze the peel over the lit match, while holding it above the cocktail and taking care to avoid the flames. Discard the strip of orange peel.

3. Garnish with the olive and enjoy.

GLASSWARE: Rocks glass

GARNISH: Strip of lemon peel

BLACK NEGRONI

A potent aperitif build around the enigmatic character of Fernet-Branca.

1½ oz. gin

1 oz. Carpano antica formula sweet vermouth

½ oz. Fernet-Branca

---

1. Place a large ice cube in the rocks glass and build the cocktail in it, adding the ingredients in the order they are listed. Stir until chilled.

2. Express the strip of lemon peel over the cocktail, garnish the cocktail with it, and enjoy.

EVEN A TREE CAN SHED TEARS

Infusing gin with an extra helping of botanicals pushes its piney character into the background, making room for other intriguing elements to surface.

1¼ oz. Herb-Infused Tanqueray No. Ten (see recipe)

½ oz. Mistia Muscat liqueur

2 bar spoons Fauchon tea liqueur

1 bar spoon fresh lemon juice

---

1. Place all of the ingredients in a cocktail shaker, fill it two-thirds of the way with ice, and shake vigorously until chilled.

2. Strain into the cocktail glass, garnish with the strip of lime peel, and enjoy.

HERB-INFUSED TANQUERAY NO. TEN: Take a fistful of herbs—half chamomile blossoms and half a mix of peppermint, cardamom, and lemongrass is a good place to start—and place it in a large mason jar. Add a 750 ml bottle of Tanqueray No. Ten gin and steep for 6 hours. Strain before using or storing.

KIWI ABSINTHE GIMLET

The green notes of kiwi suit absinthe surprisingly well.

---

1 kiwi, halved

1⅕ oz. gin

½ oz. absinthe

1 bar spoon fresh lime juice

1 bar spoon Simple Syrup (see page 26)

---

1. Squeeze the juice of the kiwi into a cocktail shaker, straining the juice through cheesecloth.

2. Add the remaining ingredients and ice and shake vigorously until chilled.

3. Strain into the cocktail glass and enjoy.

GLASSWARE: Lightbulb glass, snifter

GARNISH: Purple shiso leaf, LED ice cubes, dried electric daisy

ELECTRIC EARL

This psychedelic cocktail creates a balance between bitter flavors, from the Lady Grey–infused liqueur and grapefruit juice, and herbal freshness. Do your best to track down the dried electric daisy, too—it actually does zap your tongue.

1¾ oz. Sansho-Infused Gin (see recipe)

½ oz. fresh lime juice

⅞ oz. fresh pink grapefruit juice

3 dashes of Electric bitters

2 teaspoons Lady Grey–Infused Fortunella (see recipe)

1½ oz. Gibson Grass Cordial (see recipe)

Splash of shiso vinegar

1. Place all of the ingredients in a mixing glass, fill it two-thirds of the way with ice and, using another mixing glass, pour the cocktail back and forth between the glasses three times; the more distance between your glasses, the better. This method of mixing is known as the Cuban roll.

2. Pour the contents of the mixing glass into the chosen glassware, garnish with the purple shiso leaf, LED ice cubes, and electric daisy, and enjoy.

SANSHO-INFUSED GIN: Place ½ oz. chopped sansho pepper and a 750 ml bottle of Oxley gin in a large mixing glass and let it steep for 3 to 5 days. Strain before using or storing.

LADY GREY–INFUSED FORTUNELLA: Place 6 oz. looseleaf Lady Grey tea and a 500 ml bottle of Fortunella golden orange liqueur in a large mason jar and steep for 30 to 45 minutes. Strain before using or storing.

GIBSON GRASS CORDIAL: Place 25 oz. tonic water in a saucepan and bring it to a boil. Add 1 small handful of each of the following: loose-leaf kukicha tea, prunella leaves, shiso leaves, eucalyptus leaves, chopped lemongrass, kaffir lime leaves, lemon balm leaves, and lemon thyme leaves, reduce the heat to medium-low, and simmer for 15 minutes. Strain and add 26½ oz. sugar to the mixture. Stir until the sugar has dissolved and let the cordial cool completely before using or storing.

A cocktail featuring all of gin's potential flavor profiles: citrus, floral, spicy, and sweet.

1½ oz. gin

¾ oz. fresh lemon juice

⅞ oz. Honey Beer Syrup (see recipe)

½ oz. Drambuie

Dash of chili oil

2 drops of orange blossom honey

1 egg white

---

1. Place all of the ingredients in a cocktail shaker and dry shake for 15 seconds.

2. Add ice and shake vigorously until chilled.

3. Double strain into the coupe, garnish with the bee pollen and fresh lavender, and enjoy.

HONEY BEER SYRUP: Place 1½ cups honey beer (Honey Brown is the most popular example of a honey beer), 1 cup sugar, and ½ cup honey in a saucepan and bring to a simmer, stirring until the sugar has dissolved. Remove from hea and let cool before using or storing.

GLASSWARE: Rocks glass
GARNISH: Orange twist

CHINOTTO NEGRONI

An extra bit of bitterness from the chinotto liqueur and added brightness from the lemon juice results in a crisp and drinkable variation on the old favorite.

⅞ oz. Beefeater gin

⅞ oz. Campari

½ oz. Carpano rosso classico sweet vermouth

½ oz. Quaglia chinotto liqueur

1 teaspoon fresh lemon juice

---

1. Place all of the ingredients in a mixing glass, fill it two-thirds of the way with ice, and stir until chilled.

2. Strain over ice into a rocks glass, garnish with the orange twist, and enjoy.

GLASSWARE: Ceramic mug
GARNISH: Shiso leaf

MASCARON

The sweet sake battles the bitter sharpness of the wasabi tincture to a standstill, and creating a thoroughly enjoyable balance.

1⅜ oz. Ki No Bi Kyoto dry gin

¾ oz. Akashi-Tai Daiginjo sake

2 teaspoons Miso Shrub (see recipe)

3 drops of Wasabi Tincture (see recipe)

Lemon oil, to mist

1 piece of mackerel sashimi

Soy sauce, to taste

---

1. Place the gin, sake, and shrub in the ceramic mug and stir to combine.

2. Add the Wasabi Tincture and spritz the cocktail with lemon oil.

3. Use a brush to coat the mackerel sashimi with soy sauce. Garnish the cocktail with the shiso leaf and serve the sashimi on the side.

MISO SHRUB: Place 10½ oz. water, 10½ oz. white wine vinegar, 10 ½ oz. sugar, and 3½ oz. white miso paste in a saucepan and warm over high heat, stirring until everything has dissolved. Remove the pan from heat and let the shrub cool before using or storing.

WASABI TINCTURE: Place ¾ oz. freshly grated wasabi, 1 teaspoon wasabi paste, and 7 oz. of 88 percent alcohol spirit in a mason jar and stir to combine. Strain before using or storing. Some of this tincture would be lovely mixed into the soy sauce used on the mackerel sashimi.

and coffee.

⅞ oz. Mór Irish gin

2 teaspoons Victory gin

¾ oz. Cocchi vermouth di Torino

2 teaspoons Suze

1 teaspoon Picon Amer

2 dashes of Angostura bitters

---

1. Chill the coupe in the freezer.

2. Place all of the ingredients in a mixing glass, fill it two thirds of the way with ice, and stir until chilled.

3. Strain into the chilled coupe, garnish with the strip of orange peel, and enjoy.

PALO SANTO GIMLET

An easy-to-drink yet complex cocktail that taps into the otherworldly powers palo santo holds—it literally means "holy wood."

1¾ oz. craft gin

½ oz. fino sherry

½ oz. Lillet

½ oz. Palo Santo Cordial (see recipe)

---

1. Place all of the ingredients in a mixing glass, fill it two-thirds of the way with ice, and stir until chilled.

2. Strain over a large ice cube into the chosen glass, garnish with the lemon twist, and enjoy.

PALO SANTO CORDIAL: Place 2 teaspoons palo santo extract, 5 cups sugar, 5 teaspoons citric acid, and 5 cups water in a saucepan and warm the mixture over medium heat, stirring to dissolve the sugar; don't let the mixture come to a simmer. Once the sugar has dissolved, remove the pan from heat and let it cool completely before using or storing.

SLEEPING LOTUS

Orgeat (it's pronounced "ore-zha") is a French almond-based syrup that is available at most liquor stores and supermarkets, but a homemade version is best—not as sweet, more complex.

---

3 fresh mint leaves

2 oz. gin

1 oz. Orgeat (see recipe)

¾ oz. fresh lemon juice

2 dashes of orange bitters

---

1.   Place the mint leaves in a cocktail shaker and muddle.

2.   Add the remaining ingredients and ice and shake vigorously until chilled.

3.   Fill the Collins glass with crushed ice and double strain the cocktail over it.

4.   Garnish with the fresh mint and edible flower and enjoy.

ORGEAT: Preheat the oven to 400°F. Place 2 cups almonds on a baking sheet, place them in the oven, and toast until they are fragrant, about 5 minutes. Remove the almonds from the oven and let them cool completely. Place the almonds in a food processor and pulse until they are a coarse meal. Set the almonds aside. Place 1 cup Demerara Syrup (see page 36) in a saucepan and warm it over medium heat. Add the almond meal, remove the pan from heat, and let the mixture steep for 6 hours. Strain the mixture through cheesecloth and discard the solids. Stir in 1 teaspoon orange blossom water and 2 oz. vodka and use immediately or store in the refrigerator.

GLASSWARE: Collins glass

GARNISH: None

VIOLET FIZZ

A luscious, tropical, and eye-catching fizz that's guaranteed to please!

---

2 oz. gin

¾ oz. fresh lemon juice

½ oz. crème de violette

¼ oz. Orgeat (see page 57)

¼ oz. Rich Simple Syrup (see recipe)

½ oz. egg white

¼ oz. Passion Fruit Syrup (see recipe)

¼ oz. blue curaçao

1 oz. sparkling water, chilled, to top

---

1. Place all of the ingredients, except for the sparkling water, in a cocktail shaker and dry shake for 10 seconds.

2. Add ice and shake vigorously until chilled.

3. Double strain over 2 ice cubes into the Collins glass, top with the sparkling water, and enjoy.

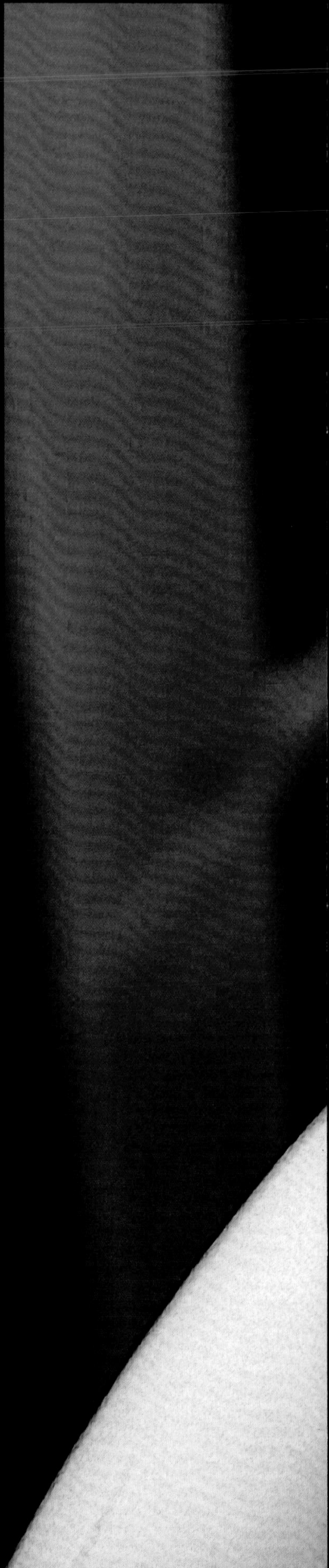

RICH SIMPLE SYRUP: Place 2 cups sugar and 1 cup water in a saucepan and bring it to a boil, stirring to dissolve the sugar. Remove the pan from heat and let the syrup cool completely before using or storing.

PASSION FRUIT SYRUP: Place 1½ cups passion fruit puree and 1½ cups Demerara Syrup (see page 36) in a mason jar, seal it, and shake until combined. Use immediately or store in the refrigerator.

GLASSWARE: Cocktail glass

GARNISH: Strip of lemon peel

LOOKING FOR YOU

Distilled from Austria's famed Klosterneuburger apricots, Rothman & Winter is far and away the best choice when ap cot liqueur or apricot brandy is called for in a cocktail recip

---

1½ oz. Aria Portland dry gin

¾ oz. Rothman & Winter orchard apricot liqueur

¾ oz. fresh lemon juice

2 dashes of Angostura bitters

---

1. Chill the cocktail glass in the freezer.

2. Place all of the ingredients in a cocktail shaker, fill it two-thirds of the way with ice, and shake vigorously until chilled.

3. Strain into the chilled cocktail glass, garnish with the str of lemon peel, and enjoy.

HAVE A HEART

Punsch, a style of liqueur popular in Sweden and other Nordic countries, used to be an important part of many cocktails, but largely disappeared because of Prohibition. This cocktail will go a long way toward putting it back in the spotlight.

1½ oz. Aria Portland dry gin

¾ oz. punsch

¾ oz. fresh lime juice

¼ oz. Grenadine (see recipe)

---

1. Chill the cocktail glass in the refrigerator.

2. Place all of the ingredients in a cocktail shaker, fill it two-thirds of the way with ice, and shake vigorously until chilled.

3. Strain into the chilled cocktail glass, garnish with the cherry, and enjoy.

GRENADINE: Place 2 cups 100 percent pomegranate juice in a saucepan and bring it to a simmer over medium-low heat. Cook until it has reduced by half. Add 2 cups sugar and stir until it has dissolved. Remove the pan from heat and let the grenadine cool completely before using or storing in the refrigerator.

PLUM COCKTAIL

Sumomo plums are usually sold as Japanese plums, Chinese plums, or Asian plums in English-speaking countries.

---

2 sumomo plums

1 oz. Tanqueray gin

1 oz. cranberry juice

1 bar spoon Grenadine (see page 61)

---

1. Squeeze the juice of the plums into a cocktail shaker, straining the juice through cheesecloth.

2. Add the remaining ingredients and ice and shake vigorously until chilled.

3. Strain into the cocktail glass and enjoy.

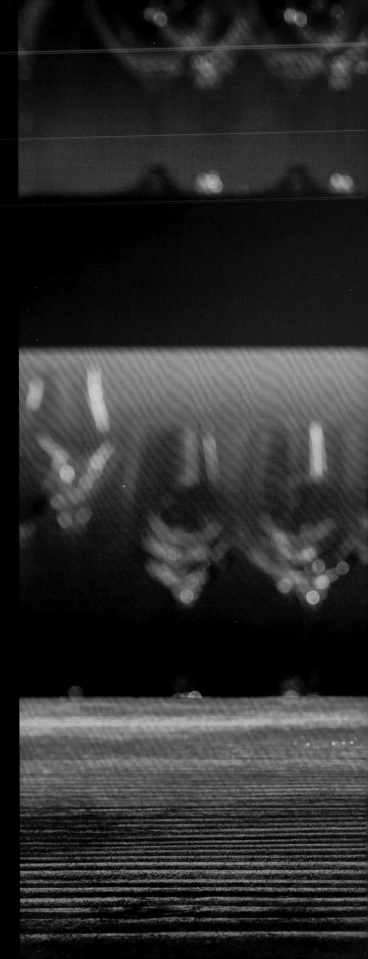

GLASSWARE: Cocktail glass

GARNISH: None

MONSIEUR L'OSIER

The vivid green color may be a throwback to an era when cocktails featured sugary, processed ingredients, but in truth the taste is timeless.

1⅓ oz. gin

2 bar spoons green tea liqueur

2 bar spoons fresh lime juice

---

1. Place all of the ingredients in a cocktail shaker, fill it two-thirds of the way with ice, and shake vigorously until chilled.

2. Strain into the cocktail glass and enjoy.

CRYSTAL GAZPACHO

A cocktail that's every bit as refreshing as the soup of the same name, and which provides a look at the culinary world's increasing influence on mixology.

---

1 oz. Tomato Gin (see recipe)

2 bar spoons Bread St-Germain (see recipe)

2 bar spoons Noilly Prat dry vermouth

½ oz. Tomato Shrub (see recipe)

1⅓ oz. tonic water

1 oz. soda water

---

1. Place gin, St-Germain, vermouth, and shrub in a cocktail shaker and dry shake for 15 seconds.

2. Pour over ice into the wineglass and top with the tonic water and soda water.

3. Garnish with the cucumber slice, fresh rosemary, slices of cherry tomato, and olive oil and enjoy.

TOMATO GIN: Place 6 cherry tomatoes and 1 cup Beefeater 24 gin in a blender and puree until smooth. Pour the mixture into a mason jar and chill in the refrigerator for 3 hours. Strain through a coffee filter before using or storing.

BREAD ST-GERMAIN: Place 1 oz. of French bread and 7 oz. St-Germain in a vacuum bag, vacuum seal it, and sous-vide at 140°F for 2 hours. Remove the vacuum bag from the water bath and let the mixture cool completely. Strain through a coffee filter before using or storing.

TOMATO SHRUB: Place 5 tomatoes in a blender and puree until smooth. Strain the puree through a coffee filter until you have 10 oz. of tomato water, leaving the puree overnight if necessary. Place the tomato water and 5 oz. sugar in a saucepan and bring it to a simmer over low heat, stirring to dissolve the sugar. Cook for 5 minutes, stir in a splash of white balsamic vinegar, and let the shrub cool completely before using or storing.

LAPSANG SOUCHONG

A smoky tea cocktail that requires much precision and advanced equipment, but is well worth the effort and investment.

---

60 ml gin

11 ml Calvados

15 ml Simple Syrup (see page 26)

180 ml water

13 g applewood chips

11 g almonds

8 g loose-leaf lapsang souchong tea

1 lemon peel

1 orange peel

1 apple slice

Pinch of chopped fresh rosemary

---

1. Place all of the liquids in the bowl of a coffee siphon. Place the remaining ingredients in the upper chamber and gently brew for 2 minutes.

2. Pour the drink into a Hot Toddy glass and enjoy.

NOTE: Only metric measurements are used in this recipe to honor its precision.

MISTER NINE

Bourbon and gin are two bold spirits that need a lot of help when asked to share space, and the St-Germain, jasmine, and bay leaf are up to the task, softening those two bruisers with their refreshing herbal natures.

---

1 oz. Jasmine-Infused Gin (see recipe)

½ oz. bourbon

½ oz. St-Germain

---

1. Place a large ice cube in the rocks glass and build the cocktail in it, adding the ingredients in the order they are listed.

2. Stir to combine, garnish with the bay leaf, and enjoy.

JASMINE-INFUSED GIN: Place 1 teaspoon loose-leaf jasmine tea and 700 ml gin in a mason jar and steep for 1 minute. Strain before using or storing.

GLASSWARE: Collins glass

GARNISH: 2 or 3 nori sheets, shredded

SEA COLLINS

The automatic sea gin from Oakland Spirits Company serves as the drink's briny anchor, packed with notes of foraged nori, lemongrass, and some other elements of California's coastal terroir.

---

2 oz. Oakland Spirits Company automatic sea gin

¾ oz. Seaweed-Infused Honey (see recipe)

½ oz. fresh lemon juice

½ oz. fresh lime juice

4 dashes of chamomile tincture

Soda water, to top

---

1. Place all of the ingredients, except for the soda water, in a cocktail shaker, fill it two-thirds of the way with ice, and shake vigorously until chilled.

2. Double strain into the Collins glass, top with soda water, and gently stir.

3. Garnish with the shredded nori and enjoy.

SEAWEED-INFUSED HONEY: Place ½ cup honey and ½ cup water in a mason jar and stir until well combined. Add dried nori and let the mixture sit at room temperature. Strain before using or storing, making sure to press down on the nori to extract as much liquid and flavor as possible.

GLASSWARE: Collins glass
GARNISH: Lemon twist

THE BEEHIVE

Adding the subtle bite of ginger and the nostalgia-evoking flavor of sarsaparilla to the Bee's Knees is a stroke of sheer brilliance.

1 oz. soda water

1½ oz. The Botanist Islay dry gin

¾ oz. fresh lemon juice

¾ oz. Ginger Solution (see recipe)

½ oz. Sarsaparilla-Infused Honey Syrup (see recipe)

2 dashes of orange bitters

2 dashes of 5 percent Saline Solution (see recipe)

1. Pour the soda water into the Collins glass.

2. Place the remaining ingredients in a cocktail shaker, fill it two-thirds of the way with ice, and shake vigorously until chilled.

3. Strain into the glass and add ice.

4. Garnish with the lemon twist and enjoy.

GINGER SOLUTION: Place ½ cup hot water, ½ cup evaporated cane sugar, and freshly pressed ginger juice in a mason jar, stir until the sugar has dissolved, and enjoy.

SARSAPARILLA-INFUSED HONEY SYRUP: Place 2 cups local honey, 1 cup hot water, and 1 oz. Indian sarsaparilla in a mason jar and stir to combine. Let the mixture steep for 24 hours. Strain before using or storing in the refrigerator.

5 PERCENT SALINE SOLUTION: Place ½ oz. of salt in a measuring cup. Add warm water until you reach 10 oz. and the salt has dissolved. Let the solution cool before using or storing.

PERFECT STRANGER

If you can get past the novelty of using goat's milk, you'll fin
a wonderful clarified milk punch has an irresistible balance
of subtle spice and sweetness.

1½ oz. Fords gin

¾ oz. Lo-Fi dry vermouth

¼ oz. Lustau oloroso sherry

½ oz. fresh lemon juice

¼ oz. fresh lime juice

½ oz. Simple Syrup (see page 26)

¼ oz. pickled jalapeño brine

2 dashes of celery bitters

Pinch of kosher salt

Goat's milk, as needed

1. Place all of the ingredients, except for the goat's milk, in
   mixing glass and stir to combine.

2. Add the goat's milk, about one-fifth of the total amount
   in the mixing glass. Stir to combine and then strain the
   mixture through cheesecloth into a jar.

3. Rinse off the cheesecloth and strain the mixture again.

4. Pour over ice into the rocks glass over ice, garnish with
   lemon twist and lime twist, and enjoy.

SIMPLY RED

A drink that features everything the modern cocktail should strive to be thoughtful, playful, tasty, and straightforward.

---

2 oz. Zephyr gin

1 oz. Simply Red Syrup (see recipe)

½ oz. fresh lime juice

¾ oz. egg whites

3 dashes of Old-Fashioned bitters

---

1. Place all of the ingredients in a cocktail shaker and dry shake for 10 seconds.

2. Add ice to the shaker and shake vigorously until chilled.

3. Double strain into the coupe, garnish with the fresh dill sprig and cinnamon, and enjoy.

SIMPLY RED SYRUP: Place 1 cup Dill Syrup (see recipe) and 1 cup pomegranate juice in a mason jar and stir to combine. Add 1 teaspoon sumac and ½ teaspoon ground Urfa pepper and steep for 15 minutes. Strain before using or storing.

DILL SYRUP: Place 2 cups water in a saucepan and bring it to a boil. Remove the pan from heat, add 5 sprigs of fresh dill, and steep for 4 minutes. Strain, add 2 cups sugar, and stir until the sugar has dissolved. Let the syrup cool completely before using or storing.

GLASSWARE: Cocktail glass
GARNISH: Carrot frond

NIGHT VISION

A brief rest in American white oak gives Spirit Works barrel gin spicy, floral, and dark fruit notes.

1½ oz. Spirit Works barrel gin

1 oz. Fresh Carrot Juice Syrup (see recipe)

½ oz. fresh lemon juice

¼ oz. Bordiga extra dry vermouth

2 dashes of oloroso sherry

2 dashes of Caraway Tincture (see recipe)

---

1. Chill the cocktail glass in the freezer.

2. Place all of the ingredients in a cocktail shaker, fill it two-thirds of the way with ice, and shake vigorously for 15 seconds.

3. Double strain into the chilled cocktail glass, garnish with the carrot frond, and enjoy.

FRESH CARROT JUICE SYRUP: Place 1 cup freshly pressed carrot and ½ cup Simple Syrup (see page 26) in a mason jar, stir to combine, and use as desired.

CARAWAY TINCTURE: Place 2 tablespoons caraway seeds and 4 oz. high-proof neutral grain alcohol in a mason jar and steep for at least 24 hours, shaking periodically. Strain before using or storing.

BOTANICAL GARDEN SPRITZ

A swarm of floral and herbal notes make this one as pleasant as a green house in the middle of winter, a burst of life in an otherwise desolate space.

¾ oz. Bloom gin

¾ oz. Belsazar white vermouth

¾ oz. Kamm & Sons British aperitif

¼ oz. St-Germain

4 drops of Dr. Adam Elmegirab's dandelion & burdock bitters

2 oz. soda water

---

1. Place all of the ingredients in a cocktail shaker, fill it two-thirds of the way with ice, and shake vigorously until chilled.

2. Strain over ice into the wineglass, garnish with the fresh dill, cucumber ribbon, and edible flowers, and enjoy.

GIN-GIN MULE

This gingery cocktail was created by the massively influential Audrey Saunders as a gateway gin drink for vodka lovers. Not only did it succeed, it inspired many variations around the world. Here is the recipe with her very own specs, including her recipe for a homemade ginger beer.

¾ oz. fresh lime juice

1 oz. Simple Syrup (see page 26)

1 sprig of fresh mint

1 oz. Homemade Ginger Beer (see recipe)

1¾ oz. Tanqueray gin

1. Place the lime juice, syrup, and mint in a mixing glass and muddle.

2. Add the ginger beer, gin, and ice and shake vigorously until chilled.

3. Strain over ice into the Collins glass, garnish with the fresh mint, lime wheel, and crystallized ginger, and enjoy.

HOMEMADE GINGER BEER

Says Saunders: "The trick is the homemade ginger beer . . . because the store-bought stuff has a peppery (more than gingery) profile—and many times insipid." Still, "if you've absolutely got to go there and use the canned stuff, then reduce the simple syrup in the drink down to ½ ounce (or less, depending on how sweet the canned stuff is)." This is for a large batch, and should make about 1 gallon.

---

1 gallon water

1 lb. fresh ginger, chopped

4 oz. light brown sugar

2 oz. fresh lime juice

---

1. Place the water in a large pot and bring to a boil.

2. Add a cup of the boiling water to a food processor along with the ginger. Blitz until the mixture is almost mulch-like.

3. Place the ginger mixture in the boiling water, turn off the heat, and stir until well combined. Cover the pot and let the mixture steep for 1 hour.

4. Strain the mixture through a chinois, pressing down on the ginger to extract as much liquid and flavor from it as possible. Stir in the brown sugar and lime juice and let the ginger beer cool before carbonating and storing in the refrigerator.

ROSE PARADE

After being distilled, Martin Miller's gin is shipped to Iceland, where it is blended with glacial spring water. If that sounds like little more than a slick bit of marketing, you obviously haven't tried it—these folks know what they're doing.

---

1 oz. Martin Miller's gin

1 oz. Cocchi Americano Rosa

½ oz. fresh lemon juice

½ oz. Giffard black rose liqueur

¼ oz. Honey Syrup (see recipe)

---

1. Place all of the ingredients in a cocktail shaker, fill it two-thirds of the way with ice, and shake vigorously until chilled.

2. Strain over ice into the rocks glass, garnish with the dried rosebuds, and enjoy.

HONEY SYRUP: Place 1½ cups water in a saucepan and bring it to a boil. Add 1½ cups honey and cook until it is just runny. Remove the pan from heat and let the syrup cool before using or storing.

GLASSWARE: Vintage teacup

GARNISH: None

LOCAL TEA PARTY

A tropical tea cocktail that you'll want to drink all summer.

---

2 oz. The Botanist gin

¾ oz. Lychee-Infused Honey (see recipe)

¾ oz. fresh lemon juice

¼ oz. Blackberry-Infused Salers Aperitif (see recipe)

1 sprig of fresh rosemary

1 bar spoon Green Chartreuse

---

1. Place the gin, honey, lemon juice, and infused aperitif in a cocktail shaker, fill it two-thirds of the way with ice, and shake vigorously until chilled.

2. Place the fresh rosemary sprig in the teacup, add the spoonful of Chartreuse, and then ignite the Chartreuse.

3. Double strain the cocktail into the teacup and enjoy.

LYCHEE-INFUSED HONEY: Place 2 cups chopped lychees, 1 cup local honey, and 1 cup water in a saucepan and bring to a simmer over low heat. Cook for 30 minutes. Remove the pan from heat and let the mixture steep for 3 hours. Strain before using or storing.

BLACKBERRY-INFUSED SALERS APERITIF: Place 2 pints of fresh blackberries and a 750 ml bottle of Salers Aperitif in a large mason jar and steep for 1 week. Strain before using or storing.

The rare cocktail that is best warm, with the blend of cilantro, chili oil, and the botanicals in the gin fusing for an exotic experience.

1½ oz. Bombay dry gin

¼ oz. fresh lime juice

3 oz. Soup Batch (see recipe)

1 bar spoon Cilantro Foam (see recipe)

1 fresh cilantro leaf

1 dehydrated lime slice

5 to 7 drops of chili oil

---

1. Place the gin, lime juice, and Soup Batch in the porcelain bowl and stir to combine.

2. Top with the Cilantro Foam, cilantro leaf, dehydrated lime slice, and chili oil and enjoy.

SOUP BATCH: Place 135 oz. unsweetened coconut milk, 15 cups coconut water, 2¾ cups freshly pressed galangal juice, 1¾ cups galanagal root debris (left from juicing, wrapped in cheesecloth), 1¼ cups thinly sliced lemongrass, 1¼ cups chicken broth, 1 tablespoon kosher salt, 1 tablespoon kaffir lime leaves, and 2¾ cups Scallion Syrup (see recipe) in a saucepan and bring to a boil. Simmer for 1 hour, remove the pan from heat, and let the mixture cool slightly. Strain before using or storing.

SCALLION SYRUP: Place 4 cups water, 8 cups sugar, and ½ cup minced scallions in a saucepan and bring to a boil, stirring to dissolve the sugar. Remove the pan from heat and let the mixture steep for 15 minutes. Strain the syrup and let it cool completely before using or storing.

CILANTRO FOAM: Place 1 tablespoon sucrose esters and ¾ cup Cilantro Water (see recipe) in a bowl and whisk with electric milk frother until foamy.

CILANTRO WATER: Place 4 oz. fresh cilantro and 5¼ cups water in a blender and puree until smooth. Strain before using or storing.

GLASSWARE: Rocks glass

GARNISH: Lemon twist

WHITE NEGRONI

Ginger liqueur and Grand Marnier bring delicious clarity to this twist on the Negroni.

---

1 oz. Domaine de Canton ginger liqueur

1 oz. Grand Marnier

1½ oz. Bulldog gin

---

1. Place all of the ingredients in a mixing glass, fill it two-thirds of the way with ice, and stir until chilled.

2. Strain over an ice sphere into the rocks glass, garnish with the lemon twist, and enjoy.

GLASSWARE: Champagne flute

GARNISH: Fresh basil leaf

BASILICO

The basil lends a pleasant touch of anise, while the lemon thyme allows the vermouth to articulate a sweet, citric note that complements the gin.

4 fresh basil leaves

1 oz. Tanqueray No. Ten gin

1 oz. Lemon Thyme–Infused Vermouth (see recipe)

Fever-Tree Mediterranean tonic, to top

1. Slap the basil leaves to awaken their aromatics and add them to a cocktail shaker. Fill it two-thirds of the way with ice, add the gin and vermouth, and shake vigorously until chilled.

2. Double strain into the champagne flute, add a few ice cubes, and top with the tonic.

3. Garnish with the fresh basil leaf and enjoy.

LEMON THYME–INFUSED VERMOUTH: Place 3 sprigs of fresh lemon thyme in a 700 ml bottle of Belsazar dry vermouth and steep for 24 hours. Remove the sprigs of lemon thyme before using or storing.

1⅜ oz. Kaffir Lime Leaf–Infused Gin (see recipe)

½ oz. pear brandy

½ oz. Giffard crème de rhubarbe

1 oz. cranberry juice

¾ oz. fresh lemon juice

1 egg white

---

1. Place all of the ingredients in a cocktail shaker, fill it two-thirds of the way with ice, and shake vigorously until chilled.

2. Strain into the highball glass and add ice cubes.

3. Garnish with the dehydrated lime wheel and maraschino cherry and enjoy.

KAFFIR LIME LEAF–INFUSED GIN: Place 10 to 12 kaffir lime leaves and a 750 ml bottle of gin in a large mason jar and stir vigorously for 1 minute. Steep for 12 hours and strain before using or storing.

THE BLACK LEAF

Most cocktails with a sour profile stop there, but this one has a surprising amount of depth thanks to the presence of Earl Grey in the cordial.

1⅜ oz. Copperhead black batch gin

¾ oz. Pear & Earl Grey Cordial (see recipe)

¾ oz. fresh lemon juice

1 teaspoon pear liqueur

1 egg white

---

1. Place all of the ingredients in a cocktail shaker and dry shake for 15 seconds.

2. Add ice and shake vigorously until chilled.

3. Double strain into the teacup, garnish with the dried lavender buds, and enjoy.

PEAR & EARL GREY CORDIAL: Place 35 oz. pear juice in a saucepan and cook over medium heat until it has reduced by half. Remove the pan from heat and add 2 bags of Earl Grey tea and 2 cinnamon sticks. Remove the bags of tea after 5 minutes. Remove the cinnamon sticks after another 5 minutes have passed. Add an equal amount of caster (superfine) sugar to the reduction and stir until it has dissolved. Let the cordial cool completely before using or storing.

GLASSWARE: Wineglass

GARNISH: 2 sliced strawberries, fresh basil

47 MONKEYS

Sloe berries, the fruit of the blackthorn shrub, are macerated in gin to provide the crimson color and warm, fruity taste sloe gin is known for.

---

3 strawberries

2 to 3 fresh basil leaves

⅞ oz. Monkey 47 Schwarzwald sloe gin

⅞ oz. Monkey 47 Schwarzwald dry gin

¾ oz. fresh lime juice

2 dashes of Peychaud's bitters

Perrier Jouet Rosé Champagne, to top

---

1. Place the strawberries in a cocktail shaker and muddle.

2. Slap the basil leaves to awaken the aromatics and add them to the shaker along with ice, the gins, lime juice, and bitters. Shake vigorously until chilled.

3. Double strain over ice into the wineglass.

4. Top with the Champagne, garnish with the sliced strawberries and fresh basil, and enjoy.

GLASSWARE: Highball glass

GARNISH: Shaved fresh ginger, 3 raspberries, fresh mint

THE MARYLEBONE CRUSH

A fresh, punch-like drink that flirts with becoming a fizz, packed with herbal undertones and a spicy kick.

1¾ oz. 108 gin

1¼ oz. cranberry juice

½ oz. fresh lime juice

Maison Sassy cidre brut, to top

---

1. Place all of the ingredients, except for the sparkling cider, in a cocktail shaker, fill it two-thirds of the way with ice, and shake vigorously until chilled.

2. Strain over ice into the highball glass and top with the sparkling cider.

3. Garnish with the ginger, raspberries, and fresh mint and enjoy.

THE COOLCUMBER

Refreshing, tropical, and floral, this cocktail is a can't miss in the summertime.

2⅛ oz. London dry gin

¾ oz. fresh lime juice

½ oz. freshly pressed cucumber juice

1¼ oz. lychee juice

½ oz. Bottlegreen elderflower cordial

3 dashes of cardamom bitters

---

1. Place all of the ingredients in a cocktail shaker, fill it two-thirds of the way with ice, and shake vigorously until chilled.

2. Strain over ice into the rocks glass, garnish with the fresh basil and lime wedge, and enjoy.

THYME TRAVELER

The Thyme Syrup ties everything together, highlighting the botanicals in the gin and the floral nature of the St-Germain.

---

1 cucumber ribbon

1½ oz. Bombay dry gin

½ oz. St-Germain

¾ oz. freshly pressed cucumber juice

½ oz. Thyme Syrup (see recipe)

½ oz. fresh lemon juice

Dash of Bittermens hellfire habanero shrub

---

1. Place all of the ingredients in a cocktail shaker, fill it two-thirds of the way with ice, and shake vigorously until chilled.

2. Strain over ice into the Collins glass, garnish with the fresh thyme, and enjoy.

THYME SYRUP: Place 1 cup water, 1 cup sugar, and 1 small bundle of fresh thyme in a saucepan and bring to a boil, stirring to dissolve the sugar. Remove the pan from heat and let the mixture steep for 1 hour. Strain and let the syrup cool completely before using or storing.

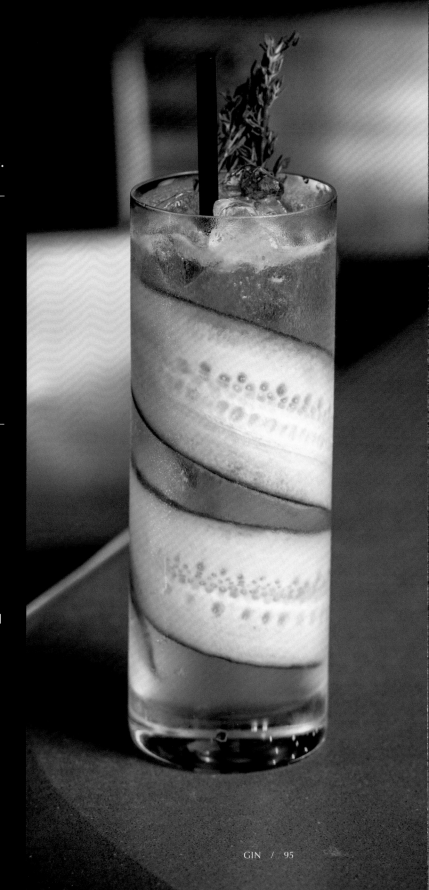

GLASSWARE: Cocktail glass

GARNISH: Lemon twist or olive

CONNAUGHT MARTINI

Though the Martini is not a "new classic," the Connaught Martini, created by Ago Perrone, the director of mixology at London's Connaught Bar, is legendary worldwide. When ordered at the hotel, it is mixed tableside, and the guest is asked to smell the aromas of each bitter (the bar offers cardamom, lavender, liquorice, grapefruit, vanilla, ginger, or coriander seed bitters, but use whatever bitters you have on hand and like best) and choose according to their preference. The signature pour is then held high above the head of the mixologist for the ultimate theatrical touch.

½ oz. dry vermouth

½ oz. Tanqueray No. Ten gin

drops of bitters

- Chill the cocktail glass in the freezer.

- Place the vermouth and gin in a mixing glass, fill it two-thirds of the way with ice, and stir until chilled.

- Coat the chilled glass with the bitters and then strain the cocktail into the glass, keeping as much distance as possible between the mixing glass and the cocktail glass.

- Garnish with the lemon twist or olive and enjoy.

GLASSWARE: Rocks glass

GARNISH: Raspberry

BRAMBLE

An invention of legendary London bartender Dick Bradsell, in his attempt to create a truly British drink.

---

2 oz. gin

1 oz. fresh lemon juice

½ oz. Simple Syrup (see page 26)

½ oz. crème de mûre

---

1. Place all of the ingredients, except for the crème de mûre, in a cocktail shaker, fill it two-thirds of the way with ice, and shake vigorously until chilled.

2. Fill the rocks glass with crushed ice and strain the cocktail over it.

3. Lace the crème de mûre on top of the drink, garnish with a raspberry, and enjoy.

GLASSWARE: Goblet

GARNISH: Edible flower

SGROPPINO PLAGIATO

There's no better way to celebrate the miracle of homemade sorbet.

Scoop of Tropical Fruit Sorbet (see recipe)

1¾ oz. Select Aperitivo

Prosecco, to top

---

1. Place the scoop of sorbet in the goblet.

2. Pour the Select Aperitivo over the sorbet and top with Prosecco.

3. Garnish with the edible flower and serve with a spoon.

TROPICAL FRUIT SORBET: Place 3½ oz. water, 3½ oz. sugar, and ½ oz. fresh lemon juice in a saucepan and bring to a simmer, stirring until the sugar has dissolved. Add the seeds of 1 vanilla bean, 14 oz. mango puree, and 3½ oz. passion fruit puree and stir until combined. Freeze for 24 hours and let sit at room temperature for 5 or 10 minutes before serving. Churn the mixture in an ice cream maker if a smoother consistency is desired.

VESCA NEGRONI

The bespoke ice is the key to this truly unique twist on the Negroni.

---

1 oz. Dolin dry vermouth

1 oz. Luxardo bitter bianco

1 oz. Fords gin

1 block of Vesca Ice (see recipe)

---

1. Place all of the ingredients, except for the Vesca Ice, in a mixing glass, fill it two-thirds of the way with ice, and stir until chilled.

2. Place the block of Vesca Ice in the rocks glass and strain the cocktail over it.

3. Garnish with the lime twist and enjoy.

VESCA ICE: Place 3½ cups, 8½ oz. aloe vera juice, 4 oz. strawberry juice, 4 oz. Sacred rosehip cup aperitif, 3 drops of MSK coconut flavouring compound, and, if desired, ½ oz. red food coloring in a large mixing bowl, stir to combine, and freeze until the mixture is solid, about 3 days. Cut into smaller blocks that will fit into a rocks glass before using.

FALLEN MADONNA

A sweet and straightforward drink with a silken texture from the aloe vera.

1¾ oz. Tanqueray gin

1¼ oz. flat tonic water

2 teaspoons fresh lemon juice

1¾ teaspoons Simple Syrup (see page 26)

⅛ oz. fresh aloe vera gel

---

1. Place all of the ingredients in a cocktail shaker, fill it two-thirds of the way with ice, and shake vigorously until chilled.

2. Strain over ice into the rocks glass, garnish with pea shoots and edible flowers, and enjoy.

LADY IN RED

A cocktail inspired by the Negroni Sbagliato, with a floral and fruity finish.

¾ oz. London dry gin

½ oz. Campari

¼ oz. Strawberry Vinegar (see recipe)

2 oz. sparkling wine

---

1. Place all of the ingredients in a mixing glass, fill it two-thirds of the way with ice, and stir until chilled.

2. Strain over a large ice cube into the coupe and enjoy.

STRAWBERRY VINEGAR: Place 10½ oz. fresh strawberries, 26 oz. apple cider vinegar, 2 whole lemons, 1 teaspoon Grenadine (see page 61), and 1½ oz. Simple Syrup (see page 26) in a mason jar and let the mixture steep for 3 days. Strain, taste to see if it is sweet enough, and add more Simple Syrup if necessary.

GLASSWARE: Coupe

GARNISH: Dehydrated lime slice, edible flowers, sprig of fresh lemon thyme, sprig of fresh lavender

PERSEPHONE

Though named after the queen of the underworld in Greek mythology, this cocktail promises to lift you up, rather than pull you down.

---

1 cucumber slice

1 fresh ginger slice

4 to 5 fresh mint leaves

1⅜ oz. No.3 London dry gin

½ oz. St-Germain

1⅜ oz. apple juice

½ oz. Fortunella golden orange liqueur

¾ oz. fresh lime juice

¾ oz. Lavender Syrup (see page 33)

1 egg white

4 dashes of lavender bitters

---

1. Place the cucumber slice, ginger slice, and mint leaves in a cocktail shaker and gently muddle.

2. Add the remaining ingredients, except for the lavender bitters, and ice and shake vigorously until chilled.

3. Double strain into the coupe and top with the lavender bitters.

4. Garnish with the dehydrated lime slice, edible flowers, and sprigs of lemon thyme and lavender and enjoy.

GLASSWARE: Custom cauldron glass or snifter

GARNISH: 1 teaspoon pea flower extract

WICCA CAULDRON CURE

The taste is not far behind, but the best feature of this potion is that the color will start changing after you've taken the first few sips.

1½ oz. Triple Citrus–Infused Gin (see recipe)

⅞ oz. fresh lemon juice

⅞ oz. Bottlegreen rhubarb & ginger cordial

1 teaspoon Ginger Syrup (see page 30)

1 oz. Moët & Chandon Champagne, to top

---

1. Place all of the ingredients, except for the Champagne, in a cocktail shaker, fill it two-thirds of the way with ice, and shake vigorously until chilled.

2. Double strain over ice into the chosen glass and top with the Champagne.

3. Just before serving, dash the pea flower extract over the top of the cocktail and enjoy without stirring.

TRIPLE CITRUS–INFUSED GIN: Place the whole peels of a lemon, orange, and a grapefruit and a 750 ml bottle of Bosford rose gin in a mason jar and steep for 24 hours. Strain before using or storing.

LONDON CALLING

A simple and classy variation on a Gin Sour so good that it has been on the cocktail menu at London's venerable Milk & Honey since it was created in 2002.

1¾ oz. gin

⅜ oz. Tio Pepe fino sherry

½ oz. fresh lemon juice

½ oz. Simple Syrup (see page 26)

2 dashes of orange bitters

---

1. Place all of the ingredients in a cocktail shaker, fill it two-thirds of the way with ice, and shake vigorously until chilled.

2. Strain into the coupe, garnish with the grapefruit twist, and enjoy.

GLASSWARE: Champagne flute
GARNISH: 3 Kalamata olives

#1 HIGH C SPRITZ

This is an opera for your palate, and probably not a bad choice to warm up your vocal cords before taking your turn on karaoke night.

---

1 oz. Olive Leaf–Infused Gin (see recipe)

2 teaspoons Nardini Acqua di Cedro

2 teaspoons Noilly Prat dry vermouth

½ teaspoon Suze saveur d'autrefois

2 oz. Three Cents gentlemen's soda

---

1. Pour all of the ingredients into a champagne flute in the order they are listed and gently stir.

2. Garnish with the Kalamata olives and enjoy.

OLIVE LEAF–INFUSED GIN: Place a 750 ml bottle of Hendrick's orbium gin and 4 oz. dried olive leaves in a mason jar and store in a cool, dark place for 5 days. Strain before using or storing.

to spirit appeals to the poet in us quite like whiskey. Immortalized in countless songs and literary works, the English writer George Bernard Shaw summed it up best when he said, "whisky is liquid sunshine." The sentiment swirling around the spirit is considerable, and very possibly spurred you to pick up this book. In reality, whiskey is the product of distillation and time. The distillation process starts with the creation of a "beer." This beer is different from what's on tap at your local, and is instead made from malted barley (Scotch), corn (bourbon), rye, wheat, or a combination of them all. The beer is brought to a boil and, since alcohol reaches its boiling point before water, that alcohol can be captured (as steam), collected, and condensed back into a liquid that will eventually become whiskey.

Whiskeys are slippery, multifaceted beasts. Even within a distinct category—bourbon, for example— there are a variety of tastes and flavors to be had. Evan Williams Single Barrel and Four Roses are both bourbons, but they do not taste the same. There are bourbons that will burn your face off—George T. Stagg, a cask-strength release that often tops 120 proof, comes to mind—and there are others that you would happily sip in your backyard. And that's just one branch of the whiskey tree. Take a quick tour through Scotch or Japanese whisky, and you will find

That said, there are some characteristics that you'll want to be knowledgeable about when using the members of the whiskey family in cocktails. Bourbon, since it is made from corn, will be slightly sweet and typically features notes of caramel and vanilla, which you'll want to draw out further, or cut against to provide complexity. Rye is dryer than bourbon, and typically features a peppery quality that goes well with citrus and the sweetness provided by many liqueurs.

Scotch, which is what most people think of the second they hear the word whiskey (even though it is called whisky, an alternative spelling utilized in Scotland, Japan, and other regions), is made and matured in Scotland using malted barley (whole grains of other cereals may be added). It must be aged in oak barrels for at least 3 years, and spirit caramel is allowed for color (unlike with bourbon).

Often, a cocktail recipe will call for Scotch as an ingredient. Fair enough, but that tells you nothing about what type of Scotch to use. Do you want a smoky single malt like an Ardbeg or a Laphroaig, or a sweeter one like a Balvenie? Or perhaps you would be wise to use a blend like Dewar's or Johnnie Walker instead? When this situation arises, you'd do well to take a brief gander at the drink's other ingredients: if they are sweet, you may want a Scotch with a bit of smoke in order to balance the cocktail. Other wise, you'll be pouring maple syrup on top of honey. Likewise, if the other ingredients are bitter or sour, a nonsmoky Scotch may be your best option. While this left-open-to-interpretation issue is most common in recipes featuring Scotch, I'd recommend a quick taste of any whiskey you are planning to mix in order to familiarize yourself with the flavors you'll be working with. When in doubt, taste.

The difficulty of working with whiskey as a cocktail ingredient has, as you might expect, elicited some amazing work from the craft cocktail movement. After all, it is dedicated to proving that anything can be put to good use if the imagination is playful enough and the execution is on point. As you'll see once you spend enough time with these recipes: wherever there seems to be the most rules is where there is actually the most freedom, the greatest chances for innovation.

BALI SPICE OLD-FASHIONED

A trio of spices grant the classic cocktail a whole new savory dimension.

---

2 oz. St. George Spirits breaking & entering bourbon

¼ oz. Bali Spice Syrup (see recipe)

Dash of Regan's orange bitters

Dash of Bitter Truth orange bitters

Zest of 1 orange

---

1. Place all of the ingredients, except for the orange zest, in a mixing glass, fill it two-thirds of the way with ice, and stir for 20 to 30 seconds.

2. Strain over one large ice cube into the rocks glass, express the orange zest over the cocktail, and discard the zest.

3. Garnish with the orange slice and enjoy.

BALI SPICE SYRUP: Break 9 inches of cinnamon sticks into small pieces. Add those pieces to a spice grinder along with 12 whole cloves and 12 star anise pods. Grind until the spices are fine, about 1 minute. Add the ground spices to a saucepan over medium heat and toast until they are aromatic, shaking the pan continually. Add 2 cups Simple Syrup (see page 26), bring to a boil, and then reduce the heat and simmer for 5 minutes. Turn off the heat and let the syrup cool for about 1 hour. Scrape the bottom of the pan to get all of the little seasoning bits and strain the syrup through a mesh strainer or chinois, using a spatula to help push the syrup through. Use immediately or store in the refrigerator.

5 pineapple chunks

1½ oz. Knob Creek bourbon

1 oz. Amaro Nonino

3 dashes of Angostura bitters

½ oz. Demerara Syrup (see page 36)

½ oz. fresh lemon juice

½ oz. pineapple juice

¾ oz. sparkling wine

---

1. Place the pineapple in a cocktail shaker and muddle it.

2. Add all of the remaining ingredients, except for the sparkling wine, fill the shaker two-thirds of the way with ice, and shake vigorously until chilled.

3. Strain into the coupe and top with sparkling wine.

4. Garnish with edible flowers and enjoy.

GLASSWARE: Rocks glass
GARNISH: None

PENICILLIN

Sam Ross dreamed up this cocktail while working at New York's famed Milk & Honey in the early aughts, and the play between the sweet spice of the syrup and the rich sweetness of blended Scotch have since sent it on a whirlwind trip around the globe.

¾ oz. Honey & Ginger Syrup (see recipe)

2 oz. blended Scotch

¾ oz. fresh lemon juice

¼ oz. smoky Islay single-malt Scotch (Laphroaig or Lagavulin recommended), to float

---

1. Place the syrup, blended Scotch, and lemon juice in a cocktail shaker, fill it two-thirds of the way with ice, and shake vigorously until chilled.

2. Strain over ice into the rocks glass. Float the single-malt Scotch on top by pouring it slowly over the back of a spoon and enjoy.

HONEY & GINGER SYRUP: Place 1 cup water, 1 cup honey, and a chopped 2-inch piece of fresh ginger in a saucepan and bring to a boil. Cook for 4 minutes, remove the pan from heat, and let the syrup cool completely. Strain before using or storing.

GLASSWARE: Rocks glass

GARNISH: Strip of orange peel

BOURBON & SPICE

The sweet, herbaceous Montenegro, spiced pear liqueur from St. George Spirits, and the spicy shrub team to produce a drink that will keep you warm all winter long.

---

1 oz. Bulleit bourbon

½ oz. Amaro Montenegro

½ oz. St. George spiced pear liqueur

Dash of Regan's orange bitters

Dash of Bittermens hellfire habanero shrub

½ teaspoon Demerara Syrup (see page 36)

---

1. Place all of the ingredients in a mixing glass, fill it two-thirds of the way with ice, and stir until chilled.

2. Strain over a large ice cube into the rocks glass, express the strip of orange peel over the cocktail, garnish the drink with the orange peel, and enjoy.

GLASSWARE: Coupe

GARNISH: Strip of orange peel

ONE WAY FLIGHT

This cocktail will carry you a long way from where you were when you started, and you'll be thrilled by not having to head back there.

1½ oz. Redwood empire rye whiskey

½ oz. cachaça

½ oz. L'Aperitivo Nonino

½ oz. Aurora Pedro Ximénez sherry

2 dashes of Angostura bitters

---

1. Place all of the ingredients in a mixing glass, fill it two-thirds of the way with ice, and stir until chilled.

2. Strain the cocktail into the coupe. Hold the strip of orange peel about 2 inches above a lit match for a couple of seconds. Twist and squeeze the peel over the lit match, while holding it above the cocktail and taking care to avoid the flames.

3. Rub the torched peel around the rim of the glass, drop it into the drink, and enjoy.

1 oz. mellow corn whiskey

1 oz. Wild Turkey rye whiskey

¾ oz. Martini & Rossi riserva speciale rubino

½ oz. Martini & Rossi bitter

1¼ oz. iced hibiscus tea

½ oz. Red Pepper Syrup (see recipe)

½ oz. Citric Acid Solution (see recipe)

---

1. Place all of the ingredients in a mixing glass and fill it two-thirds of the way with ice. Using another mixing glass, pour the cocktail back and forth between the glasses three times; the more distance between your glasses, the better. This method of mixing is known as the Cuban roll.

2. Place a large ice cube in the goblet and strain the cocktail over it.

3. Garnish with the baby corn and cornflower and enjoy.

in a saucepan and bring it to a boil. Add 2 chopped red bell peppers and 17½ oz. demerara sugar and stir until the sugar has dissolved. Remove the pan from heat and let the syrup cool completely. Pour the mixture, without straining, into a mason jar and chill it in the refrigerator overnight. Strain the syrup before using or storing.

CITRIC ACID SOLUTION: Place 10 oz. water and ½ oz. citric acid in a mason jar and stir until the citric acid has dissolved. Use as desired.

CUBISM

Fernet-Branca Menta is, as you might have intuited, Ferne
with an even stronger minty profile. But as that character
comes through more on nose than on the palate, it's a dynamic cocktail ingredient.

1 oz. Bulleit bourbon

2 teaspoons Cognac

2 teaspoons Diplomático reserva rum

2 teaspoons Simple Syrup (see page 26)

1 teaspoon Fernet-Branca Menta

1 strip of lemon zest

1. Place all of the ingredients in a mixing glass, fill it two-
   thirds of the way with ice, and stir until chilled.

2. Strain over a large ice cube into the rocks glass, apply
   the four drops of cherry gelatin just below the rim of the
   glass, making sure they are parallel to the rim, and enjo

A fusion of an Old Fashioned and a Gimlet provides a zingy and irresistible combination. Despite the name, the bourbon doesn't have to be Michter's.

1¼ oz. Pear Cordial (see recipe)

1½ oz. bourbon

2 dashes of salt

---

1. Place a large ice cube in the coupe.

2. Add the ingredients, stir until chilled, and enjoy.

PEAR CORDIAL: Place 2 oz. malic acid, 1.8 oz. citric acid, 15 cups water, 9¼ cups superfine (caster) sugar, and 3 lbs. diced Passe Crassane pears in a large container and stir to combine. Chill in the refrigerator for 24 hours. Strain the cordial through cheesecloth, stir in 1 teaspoon vodka, and use immediately or store in the refrigerator.

BANGKOK, BANGKOK

Cinnamon, nutmeg, cloves, star anise, allspice, and whatever else you like when fall hits can be used for the autumn spices in the Rye & Tea Infusion.

1½ oz. Rye & Tea Infusion (see recipe)

¾ oz. Thai Tea Reduction (see recipe)

½ oz. Meletti Amaro

1½ oz. coconut cream

2 dashes of Bittermens hopped grapefruit bitters

Toasted autumn spices, to top

---

1. Place all of the ingredients, except for the autumn spices, in a cocktail shaker, fill it two-thirds of the way with ice, and shake vigorously until chilled.

2. Fill the Collins glass with crushed ice and strain the cocktail over it.

3. Top with the autumn spices, garnish with your preferred fresh herbs, and enjoy.

RYE & TEA INFUSION: Line a coffee dripper with a paper filter and place loose-leaf Thai tea, hazelnuts, autumn spices, and dried cranberry hibiscus blossoms in the filter. Slowly pour rye whiskey and then Meletti over the mixture and use as desired.

THAI TEA REDUCTION: Place 1½ cups sugar and 1 cup water in a saucepan, add 1 ½ teaspoons loose-leaf Thai tea, and bring to a simmer. Cook until the mixture has reduced, stirring occasionally to dissolve the sugar. Remove the pan from heat and let the reduction cool completely. Strain before using or storing.

SAYONARA!

Ichijiku are Japanese figs, and kuromitsu is a Japanese sugar syrup whose name translates to "black honey." Both can be found online, or at well-stocked Asian markets.

---

2 oz. Ichijiku-Infused Whisky (see recipe)

5 drops of white soy sauce

2 dashes of Kombu & Nori Bitters (see recipe)

⅓ oz. Licorice Kuromitsu (see recipe)

---

1. Place all of the ingredients in mixing glass, fill it two-thirds of the way with ice, and stir until chilled.

2. Strain into over ice into the rocks glass, garnish with the sliced ichijiku, and enjoy.

ICHIJIKU-INFUSED WHISKY: Placed 5 halved ichijiku and a 750 ml bottle of Nikka From the Barrel whisky in a vacuum bag, vacuum seal it, and sous vide at 122°F for 1 hour. Remove the bag from the water bath and let the mixture cool. Strain before using or storing.

KOMBU & NORI BITTERS: Place a pinch of nori, a dash of kombu, and a 6.7 oz. bottle of Angostura bitters in a vacuum bag, vacuum seal it, and sous vide at 126.5°F for 2 hours. Remove the bag from the water bath and let the mixture cool. Strain before using or storing.

GLASSWARE: Hurricane glass

GARNISH: Candied pineapple wedge, Luxardo maraschino cherry, tiki umbrella

THE ROBIN'S NEST

A touch of cranberry juice makes this drink perfect for the fall, when you first feel the summer slipping away, and winter approaching.

---

1 oz. Suntory Toki Japanese Whisky

½ oz. Plantation O.F.T.D. rum

½ oz. Cinnamon Syrup (see recipe)

½ oz. fresh lemon juice

¾ oz. pineapple juice

1 oz. Passion Fruit Honey (see recipe)

1 oz. cranberry juice

---

1. Place all of the ingredients, except for the cranberry juice, in a cocktail shaker, fill it two-thirds of the way with ice, and shake vigorously until chilled.

2. Fill the Hurricane glass with crushed ice and top with the cranberry juice.

3. Garnish the cocktail with the candied pineapple wedge and maraschino cherry and enjoy.

CINNAMON SYRUP: Place 1 cup water and 2 cinnamon sticks in a saucepan and bring the mixture to a boil. Add 2 cups sugar and stir until it has dissolved. Remove the pan from heat, cover it, and let the mixture steep at room temperature for 12 hours. Strain the syrup through cheesecloth before using or storing.

PASSION FRUIT HONEY: Place 1 cup honey in a saucepan and warm it over medium heat until it is runny. Pour the honey into a mason jar, stir in 1 cup passion fruit puree, and let the mixture cool before using or storing in the refrigerator.

GLASSWARE: Cocktail glass
GARNISH: None

GRAIN MARKET

A single-grain spirit made from corn and aged in oak, Nikka grain is sweet like a bourbon, but features tropical notes and citrus rather than the vanilla you'd expect.

6 kyoho or Concord grapes

1½ oz. Nikka Coffey grain whisky

⅔ oz. medium-sweet Madeira

1. Place the grapes in a cocktail shaker and muddle.

2. Add ice, the whisky, and Madeira and shake vigorously until chilled.

3. Double strain into the cocktail glass and enjoy.

GLASSWARE: Double rocks glass
GARNISH: Grapefruit twist

BOROUGH

A smooth stirred bourbon drink that makes for the perfect nightcap.

---

2 oz. bourbon

1 oz. Punt e Mes vermouth

¼ oz. Burly cascara cola syrup

¼ oz. absinthe

2 dashes of Angostura bitters

2 dashes orange bitters

---

1. Place all of the ingredients in a mixing glass, fill it two-thirds of the way with ice, and stir until chilled.

2. Strain over a large ice cube into the rocks glass, garnish with the grapefruit twist, and enjoy.

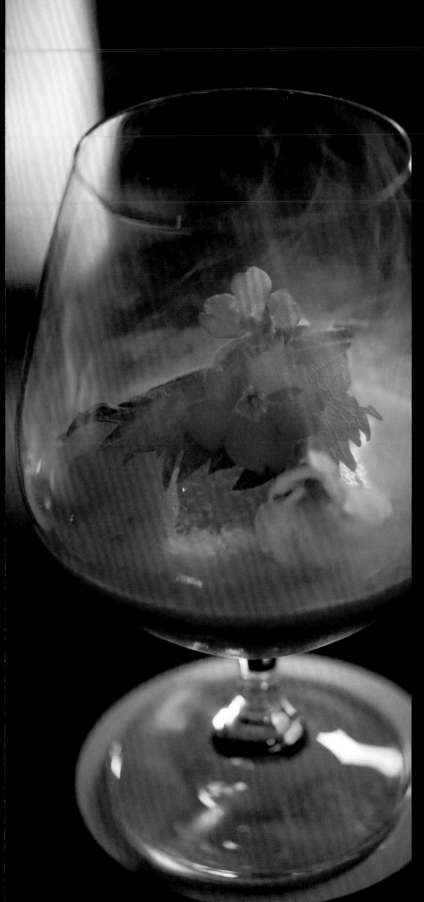

CHERRY CHERRY MONKEY

The Salted Pistachio Syrup is good enough that it can be used in just about everything. That's a lucky break, as you'll want to try using it in everything after your initial encounter

---

1½ oz. Monkey Shoulder blended Scotch whisky

1 oz. Salted Pistachio Syrup (see recipe)

½ oz. fresh lime juice

8 to 10 cherries

5 drops of shiso bitters or 1 bar spoon Dover shiso liqueur

---

1. Place all of the ingredients in a mason jar and use a han blender to emulsify the mixture.

2. Strain the mixture into a cocktail shaker, fill it two-thirds of the way with ice, and shake vigorously until chilled.

3. Strain over a large ice cube into the brandy snifter, garnish the cocktail with the shiso leaf and edible flowers, and enjoy.

SALTED PISTACHIO SYRUP: Place 3½ oz. raw pistachio meats in a dry skillet and toast them over medium heat unti they start to brown, 6 to 8 minutes. Place the toasted pistachios, 17½ oz. sugar, 25⅓ oz. water, and 1 tablespoon fine sea salt in a blender and puree until combined. Strain befor using or storing.

GLASSWARE: Rocks glass

GARNISH: Strip of orange peel

BLACK CAT

Yomeishu is a bittersweet herbal elixir sold in Japan as a remedy for fatigue, poor circulation, and gastrointestinal issues. That branding would cause most bartenders to ignore it, but it pairs brilliantly with whisky.

---

1 oz. Mars Iwai tradition whisky

½ oz. Yomeishu

½ oz. white peach liqueur

1 bar spoon fresh lemon juice

---

1. Place all of the ingredients in a cocktail shaker, fill it two-thirds of the way with ice, and shake very briefly.

2. Strain over ice into the rocks glass, garnish with the strip of orange peel, and enjoy.

GLASSWARE: Champagne flute
GARNISH: None

BELLINI 95

This mashup of a Bellini and a French 95 is rich and nutty, and requires a serious amount of practice to get the texture and complexity just right.

---

2 oz. Bellini 95 Mix (see recipe), chilled

2 oz. Champagne

---

1. Chill the Champagne flute in the freezer.

2. Pour the chilled Bellini 95 Mix into the flute.

3. Add the Champagne, lift it just once with a bar spoon, and enjoy.

BELLINI 95 MIX: Place 1 cup Wakocha-Infused Whisky (see recipe), 2 cups peach nectar, 1 cup cold-brew wakocha, ½ cup Pumpkin Seed Orgeat (see recipe), ½ cup distilled water, and 6 tablespoons fresh lemon juice in a large container and stir to combine. Place 1½ cups of the mixture in a mason jar and stir in 1 teaspoon agar agar powder. Store what remains of the mixture in the refrigerator. Place the mixture in the mason jar in a saucepan and warm it over medium heat until it starts to thicken. Remove the pan from heat, pour the mixture back into the mason jar, and chill it in the refrigerator until it is a light jelly, 2 to 3 hours. Strain before using or storing.

WAKOCHA-INFUSED WHISKY: Place 2 teaspoons loose-leaf wakocha tea and a 750 ml bottle of Dewar's 12 year Scotch whisky in a vacuum bag, vacuum seal it, and sous-vide at 125°F for 2 hours. Strain before using or storing.

PUMPKIN SEED ORGEAT: Place 7 oz. pumpkin seeds in a skillet and toast them over medium heat until lightly browned, shaking the pan occasionally. Cover the toasted seeds with water and let them soak overnight. Drain the seeds, place them in a blender, add 14 oz. water, and puree until smooth. Strain the mixture through cheesecloth, place the liquid and 1 lb. caster (superfine) sugar in a large container, and stir until the sugar has dissolved. Stir in 1 oz. of Bacardí reserve ocho rum and 3 drops of orange blossom water and use immediately or store in the refrigerator.

SHISO MISO

Enriching Japanese whisky with flavorful elements like butter, miso, and shiso makes for a spirit that has a cocktail's worth of surprises all by itself.

1¾ oz. Fat-Washed Nikka Days Whisky (see recipe)

1¾ teaspoons Demerara Syrup (see page 36)

6 dashes of Angostura bitters

---

1. Place all of the ingredients in a mixing glass, fill it two-thirds of the way with ice, and stir until chilled.

2. Strain over a large ice cube into the ceramic mug, garnish with the shiso leaf, and enjoy.

FAT-WASHED NIKKA DAYS WHISKY: Pour 1¾ cups Nikka Days whisky into a large mason jar. Place 5 tablespoons unsalted butter in a small saucepan and warm it over medium heat. Stir in ¼ oz. white miso paste and ¼ oz. fresh shiso leaves and cook until the butter starts to brown. Remove pan from heat and pour the mixture into the mason jar. Stir until thoroughly combined, seal tightly with plastic wrap, and freeze overnight. Scrape away the solidified layer of butter and strain the whisky before using or storing.

GLASSWARE: Highball glass

GARNISH: Fresh mint, freshly grated nutmeg, strip of orange peel

AMERICAN TROUBADOUR

Wild Turkey 81 and marnier

---

oz. Wild Turkey 81 bourbon

½ oz. Fernet-Branca Menta

½ oz. Grand Marnier

oz. nitro cold brew

¼ oz. Demerara Syrup (see page 36)

2 dashes of 18.21 Japanese Chili Lime Bitters

---

1. Place all of the ingredients in a cocktail shaker, fill it two-thirds of the way with ice, and shake vigorously until chilled.

2. Strain, discard the ice in the shaker, and return the cocktail to the shaker. Dry shake for 10 seconds.

3. Pour the cocktail over ice into the highball glass, garnish with the fresh mint, freshly grated nutmeg, and strip of orange peel, and enjoy.

A LA LOUISIANE

A spicier, rye-forward version of a cocktail that originated in New Orleans in the nineteenth century.

1¾ oz. rye whiskey

¾ oz. sweet vermouth

¼ oz. Benedictine

3 dashes of absinthe

3 dashes of Peychaud's Bitters

---

1. Chill the coupe in the freezer.

2. Place all of the ingredients in a mixing glass, fill it two-thirds of the way with ice, and stir until chilled.

3. Strain into the chilled coupe, garnish with the Amarena cherry, and enjoy.

GLASSWARE: Tumbler

GARNISH: Orange slice

WHISKEY GINGER

Just a pinch of fresh ginger is all that's needed to push this riff on a Kentucky Mule someplace memorable.

½ oz. Buffalo Trace bourbon

oz. Fentimans ginger beer

dashes of Peychaud's bitters

inch of grated fresh ginger

Fill the tumbler with ice and then add the bourbon, ginger beer, and bitters.

Top the cocktail with the ginger, garnish with the slice of orange, and enjoy.

SMOKE SHOW

If an even greater smoky flavor is desired here, toss some o
chips in a smoking gun and smoke the cocktail for 15 secon

---

3 oz. Knob Creek rye whiskey

⅓ oz. Grade A maple syrup

⅓ oz. water

2 dashes of Scrappy's orange bitters

Dash of Angostura bitters

---

1. Place all of the ingredients in a cocktail shaker, fill it
   two-thirds of the way with ice, and shake vigorously unt
   chilled.

2. Strain over an ice sphere into the rocks glass, garnish
   with the maraschino cherry, and enjoy.

GLASSWARE: Rocks glass

GARNISH: Dehydrated orange wheel

RING A DING DING

Powerfully spicy and complex thanks to the blend of pot still Jamaican rums that are a part of it, Hamilton pimento dram is well worth seeking out.

1½ oz. Scotch whisky

½ oz. Cointreau

½ oz. Hamilton pimento dram

½ oz. Ancho Reyes Verde poblano chile liqueur

¼ oz. Demerara Syrup (see page 36)

4 dashes of Angostura bitters

4 dashes of Fee Brothers Aztec Chocolate bitters

---

1. Place all of the ingredients in a mixing glass, fill it two-thirds of the way with ice, and stir until chilled.

2. Strain into the cocktail glass, garnish with the dehydrated orange wheel, and enjoy.

MIND MAPS

A full-bodied cocktail from the brilliant Ryan Chetiyawardana and his team at Lyaness that seeks to emphasize the pear and chocolate notes you find in certain blended Scotches, like Monkey Shoulder.

1¾ oz. blended Scotch whisky

2 teaspoons Amontillado sherry

1½ teaspoons pear liqueur

1 teaspoon white crème de cacao

1 teaspoon Cointreau

½ teaspoon Demerara Syrup (see page 36)

2 dashes of Angostura bitters

---

1. Chill the coupe in the freezer.

2. Place all of the ingredients in the coupe and stir to combine.

3. Garnish with the lemon twist and enjoy.

Q & A WITH RYAN CHETIYAWARDANA

One of the best-known names in the bartending world, Ryan Chetiyawardana (better-known as "Mr. Lyan") first shook up the industry by creating drinks in batches, without ice or citrus, in order to emphasize quality of service.

With each of his projects, he has found a new angle on how drinks are conceived and created while focusing on sustainability.

When his bar Dandelyan was declared "Best Bar" at the 2018 Tales of the Cocktail Festival, Chetiyawardana announced its closure and has since replaced it with Lyaness.

What was your mixology and entrepreneurship education before opening your first bar?

I originally started in kitchens. Over my career, I've worked in pretty much every position covering pubs, fine dining, small cocktail bars, boutique hotels, nightclubs, and five-star hotels. I've taken little bits from all of them—good and bad—but I was thankful to have some great mentors along the way. I was also able to explore lots of different sides to what I loved: hosting and creating great drinks at (Edinburgh, Scotland, bar) Bramble, running the lab and R & D at 69 Colebrooke Row, to leading the creative development of the Whistling Shop.

How does Lyaness reflect your overall philosophy to cocktail creation?

I say we create "accessible innovation," but really, we like to create beautiful and comfortable places that feel exciting for people to gather with their family and friends. But it needs to balance—although we like the weirder side of things, and something that feels different and special, we want to make sure it feels relevant and honest to people. Within each

of the venues, we're always trying to challenge and kick off a discussion. We use everything in our control to address this—the setting, the music, the lighting, the set-up for the team and, of course, the food and drink. We try and create platforms for the team to shine and with Lyaness I believe we've really hit that. It's an incredible space, but we have the best team in the world; they've created something that feels very distinct to the global drinking scene and have made it accessible to everyone—not just cocktail geeks.

You've pushed hard for sustainability initiatives in the hospitality supply chain. How does being in London affect what you do in this regard?

Sustainability has been a pillar of the company for the last 10 years and London poses some challenges and opportunities for this. In one sense, the platform, the critical mass, and the engagement mean we have a greater opportunity to instigate positive change. The growing number of kindred spirits means we can pool resources, but London still poses problems. We are removed from farmers and costs are incredibly high. So, it also poses challenges that other spaces don't have to navigate.

What makes London stand out to you as a cocktail city?

London is the most diverse city in the world, but it's also a global hub for finance, tech, fashion, and the arts, which all leads to creating the most dynamic food-and-drink scene on the planet. Coupled with the fact that people from across the world are able to work here, and are attracted to working here, it means there's an unprecedented dynamic among communities here.

BLOOD RED DIAMOND

An earthy and juicy cocktail that leans heavily upon the bright and sweet flavor Irish whiskey is known for.

1⅕ oz. Jameson Irish whiskey

½ oz. Hōjicha Honey Water (see recipe)

2 bar spoons Roasted Sweet Potato Juice (see recipe)

1 bar spoon freshly pressed beet juice

---

1. Place all of the ingredients in a mixing glass, fill it two-thirds of the way with ice, and stir until chilled.

2. Strain into the cocktail glass and enjoy.

HŌJICHA HONEY WATER: Place ½ cup honey and ½ cup freshly brewed hōjicha tea in a mason jar and stir to combine. Let the mixture cool completely before using or storing.

ROASTED SWEET POTATO JUICE: Preheat the oven to 400°F. Place 1 sweet potato in the oven and roast it until the flesh is tender, about 1 hour. Remove the sweet potato from the oven and scrape the sweet potato's flesh into a blender. Add 3 parts water and puree until smooth. Strain through cheesecloth before using or storing.

GLASSWARE: Cocktail glass

GARNISH: Cinnamon-dusted dried rosebud

LAUGH

The amazake, a low-alcohol fermented rice drink from Japan, amplifies the apple and lactic notes present in Johnnie Walker gold label.

1⅓ oz. Johnnie Walker gold label Scotch whisky

1 oz. Amazake Falernum (see recipe)

1 oz. Apple Pie Juice (see recipe)

1 bar spoon fresh lemon juice

1 bar spoon loose-leaf ruby orange tea

Dash of Bob's orange & mandarin bitters

---

1. Place all of the ingredients in a cocktail shaker, fill it two-thirds of the way with ice, and shake vigorously until chilled.

2. Strain into the cocktail glass, garnish with the cinnamon-dusted dried rosebud, and enjoy.

AMAZAKE FALERNUM: Place 1 cup amazake, 1 cup sugar, 1 cinnamon stick, ¼ vanilla bean, ½ teaspoon cardamom pods, 1 teaspoon whole cloves, 2 lemon slices, and 2 lime slices in a saucepan and bring to a simmer over medium heat, stirring to dissolve the sugar. Remove the pan from heat and let the falernum cool completely. Strain before using or storing.

APPLE PIE JUICE: Place 10 oz. apple juice, ¼ teaspoon cinnamon, and ½ vanilla bean in a saucepan and bring to a boil over medium-high heat. Cook until the mixture has reduced by half. Remove the pan from heat and let the mixture cool completely. Strain before using or storing.

GLASSWARE: Cocktail glass

GARNISH: Strawberry powder, granules of dried raspberry

IRISH BREEZE

A fruity, chilled take on Irish Coffee. Any locally roasted espresso works here, but one made from Ethiopian beans, with their winey, floral flavor, will provide the best results.

¾ oz. Teeling Irish whiskey

1½ oz. freshly brewed espresso

⅔ oz. Hibiscus Syrup (see recipe)

1½ oz. heavy cream, lightly whipped

---

1. Place the whiskey, espresso, and syrup in a mixing glass, fill it two-thirds of the way with ice, and stir until chilled.

2. Strain into the cocktail glass and float the lightly whipped cream on top by gently pouring it over the back of a spoon.

3. Garnish with strawberry powder and granules of dried raspberry and enjoy.

HIBISCUS SYRUP: Place 1 teaspoon loose-leaf hibiscus tea in 1 cup Simple Syrup (see page 26) and steep for 10 days. Strain before using or storing.

PERFECT NIKKA

If you're looking for a little more bitterness here, swap
Cocchi Americano in for the Lillet.

1⅔ oz. Nikka Coffey grain whisky

1 bar spoon Lillet

1 bar spoon Tempus Fugit crème de cacao

1 bar spoon coffee

1. Place all of the ingredients in a mixing glass, fill it two-
   thirds of the way with ice, and stir until chilled.

2. Strain into the tin bowl and enjoy.

JAPANESE OLD FASHIONED

A shiitake mushroom infusion and bitters containing kelp, bonito, and shiitake help turn the Old Fashioned into an umami bomb.

1½ oz. Shiitake-Infused Whisky (see recipe)

Dash of The Japanese Bitters umami bitters

1 bar spoon maple syrup

---

1. Place all of the ingredients in a mixing glass, fill it two-thirds of the way with ice, and stir until chilled.

2. Strain over ice into the rocks glass, garnish with the slice

GLASSWARE: Cocktail glass

GARNISH: Strip of orange peel

THE COUNTRY LAWYER

Revived after years of toiling away due to mismanagement, the subtle sweetness of Four Roses bourbon makes this memorable digestif cocktail.

1½ oz. Four Roses bourbon

½ oz. Zucca rabarbaro amaro

½ oz. Dolin dry vermouth

¼ oz. Benedictine

Dash of chocolate bitters

---

1. Place all of the ingredients in a mixing glass, fill it two-thirds of the way with ice, and stir until chilled.

2. Strain into the cocktail glass, garnish with the strip of orange peel, and enjoy.

GLASSWARE: Rocks glass

GARNISH: Sesame & Citrus Candy (see recipe)

TIME'S ARROW II

Some preparation is required for the candy garnish, but the result, both from an aesthetic and taste vantage, is worth it.

---

1 oz. Sesame-Infused Whisky (see recipe)

1 oz. Luxardo bitter bianco

1 oz. Carpano Bianco vermouth

1 bar spoon Oleo Salis (see recipe)

---

1. Place all of the ingredients in a mixing glass, fill it two-thirds of the way with ice, and stir until chilled.

2. Strain over a large ice cube into the rocks glass, garnish with the Sesame & Citrus Candy, and enjoy.

SESAME-INFUSED WHISKY: Place 1 cup toasted sesame seeds and a 750 ml bottle of Suntory Toki whisky in a mason jar and let steep for 3 days. Strain before using or storing.

OLEO SALIS: Place the zest of 10 lemons and 10 oranges in a bowl, add ½ cup kosher salt, and wearing latex gloves, work the mixture with your hands for 2 minutes. Cover and let the mixture sit overnight. Stir in 2 oz. Suntory Toki whisky and strain the liquid into a mason jar, pressing down on the solids to extract as much as possible from them.

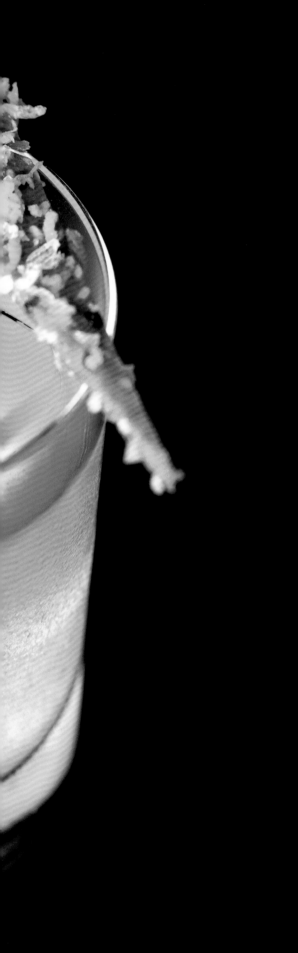

SESAME & CITRUS CANDY

You can cut the caramel into whatever shapes you like, but crosshatching in a simple rectangular pattern will yield the most usable pieces.

½ cup sugar

3 tablespoons toasted sesame seeds (mix of white and black)

Zest of 1 lemon

Zest of 1 orange

⅛ teaspoon baking soda

1 teaspoon Maldon sea salt

---

1. Line a baking sheet with parchment paper. Thinly coat a small saucepan with some of the sugar. Warm the sugar over medium-high heat and wait for it to begin melting. Gradually add more sugar to the spots in the pan where the sugar is liquefying. Once about a third of the sugar has been introduced, the pace of adding the sugar can be increased. When all of the sugar has been added, stir it with a wooden spoon until it has caramelized.

2. Add the sesame seeds, lemon zest, orange zest, and baking soda and stir until thoroughly combined.

3. Pour the mixture onto the parchment-lined baking sheet and use an offset spatula to spread the caramel in a thin layer.

4. While the caramel is still hot, sprinkle the salt over the surface. Let the caramel cool for 1 minute.

5. Use a sharp knife to score the firm, yet slightly tacky, caramel candy in whatever shapes you like.

6. Wait for the caramel to set fully before breaking it along the score marks.

GLASSWARE: Julep cup

GARNISH: Fresh mint, blackberries

BLACKBERRY DERBY

Using sunflower seeds to add a rich, nutty note to the bourbon keeps the shrub from running away with the flavor of this cocktail.

---

8 to 10 fresh mint leaves

½ oz. Blackberry & Honey Shrub (see recipe)

2 oz. Sunflower Seed–Infused Bourbon (see recipe)

2 dashes of Angostura bitters

---

1. Place the mint leaves and shrub in the Julep cup and muddle.

2. Add the bourbon and crushed ice and stir until the outside of the cup is nicely frosted.

3. Top with more crushed ice and the bitters, garnish with the fresh mint and blackberries, and enjoy.

BLACKBERRY & HONEY SHRUB: Place 1 cup clover honey in a saucepan and warm it over medium heat for approximately 5 minutes. Add 1 cup Lucero Blackberry Red Balsamic Vinegar and stir continually for 1 minute. Remove the pan from heat, add 1 cup room-temperature water, and let the shrub cool completely before using or storing.

SUNFLOWER SEED–INFUSED BOURBON: Place 4 cups bourbon and ½ cup salted sunflower seeds in a container and steep for 8 to 16 hours. Strain before using or storing.

TABLE 32

Macerating the berries for 1 week allows them to ferment just slightly, adding a pleasant funk without overcomplicating this serve via other spirits.

---

2 oz. Old Forester bourbon

2 oz. Macerated Berries (see recipe)

1 oz. fresh lime juice

½ oz. Orgeat (see page 57)

Soda water, to top

---

1. Place all of the ingredients, except for the soda water, in a cocktail shaker, fill it two-thirds of the way with ice, and shake vigorously until chilled.

2. Strain over ice into the Collins glass, garnish with fresh mint and edible flowers, and enjoy.

MACERATED BERRIES: Place 1 cup blueberries, 1 cup sliced strawberries, 1 cup raspberries, 3 tablespoons Old Forester bourbon, and 1 tablespoon sugar in a bowl and stir gently until all ingredients are mixed. Let the mixture macerate in the refrigerator for 1 week. Strain off the liquid and store the berries in the refrigerator.

Fat-washing is a great way of adding another dimension to spirits, giving them an irresistible depth.

1⅜ oz. Fat-Washed Ragtime Rye Whiskey (see recipe)

¾ oz. red date tea

1 teaspoon Sichuan Peppercorn Syrup (see recipe)

1 teaspoon crème de peche

3 drops of vanilla bitters

Hay, for smoking

---

1. Place all of the ingredients, except for the hay, in a mixing glass, fill it two-thirds of the way with ice, and stir until chilled.

2. Strain over frozen whiskey stones into the rocks glass.

3. Fill a smoking gun with hay and smoke the cocktail for 10 to 15 seconds.

4. Garnish with the sesame cracker and edible butterfly and enjoy.

FAT-WASHED RAGTIME RYE WHISKEY: Place 1⅞ oz. sesame oil and a 750 ml bottle of Ragtime rye whiskey in a large mason jar, shake vigorously, and store in a cool, dry place for 24 hours. Place the mixture in the freezer until the oil solidifies into a solid layer. Remove the oil and strain the whiskey through cheesecloth before using or storing.

SICHUAN PEPPERCORN SYRUP: Place 9 oz. water, 9 oz. honey, and ¾ oz. Sichuan peppercorns in a saucepan and bring to a boil. Reduce the heat and let the mixture simmer for 20 minutes. Remove the pan from heat and let the mixture cool completely. Strain before using or storing.

CAOL ILA COSMO

Throwing smoky single malt in for the vodka in a Cosmo shows just how much opportunity there is when it comes to reinterpreting classic cocktails.

1⅛ oz. Caol Ila 12 year Scotch whisky

½ oz. Cointreau

⅝ oz. cranberry juice

⅝ oz. Citric Acid Solution (see page 118)

---

1. Chill the Nick & Nora glass in the freezer.

2. Add all of the ingredients to the chilled glass, stir to com bine, and enjoy.

EARL OF SEVILLE

A multilayered drink with an emphasis on subtle citrus touches.

1¾ oz. Earl Grey–Infused Chivas Regal (see recipe)

⅛ oz. fresh lemon juice

1 teaspoon Italicus rosolio di bergamotto liqueur

1 teaspoon Demerara Syrup (see page 36)

½ teaspoon Fernet-Branca

1 tablespoon bitter orange marmalade

Apple Foam (see recipe), to top

---

1. Chill the Nick & Nora glass.

2. Place all of the ingredients, except for the Apple Foam, in a cocktail shaker and shake vigorously until chilled.

3. Double strain into the chilled glass and top with the Apple Foam.

4. Garnish with the dehydrated apple slice and enjoy.

EARL GREY–INFUSED CHIVAS REGAL: Place 1¾ cups Chivas Regal 12 year whisky and 3 bags of Earl Grey tea (or ⅛ oz. loose-leaf) in a mason jar and steep for 30 minutes. Remove the tea bags before using or storing.

APPLE FOAM: Place 14 oz. apple juice, ⅛ oz. egg white powder, and 2 teaspoons Demerara Syrup in a whipping gun and use 1 charge to whip until the mixture is foamy.

GLASSWARE: Rocks glass

GARNISH: Half a miniature Snickers bar

THE MARATHON MAN

A birthday cake in a glass, and just as filling.

---

1 oz. FEW bourbon

¾ oz. Kahlúa

2 teaspoons Orgeat (see page 57)

¾ oz. Frangelico

¾ oz. Mozart dark chocolate liqueur

1 tablespoon peanut butter

1½ oz. whole milk

1 miniature Snickers bar

---

1. Place all of the ingredients to a blender along with two large ice cubes and pulse until there are fine bubbles throughout and the ice has been thoroughly incorporated.

2. Pour over ice into the rocks glass, garnish with the Snickers bar, and enjoy.

GLASSWARE: Goblet

GARNISH: Dark chocolate or walnuts, on the side

NIGHT BLAZE

If done correctly, the rich fruits from the Glenmorangie and the plum sake will be followed by a lovely finish that features smoke from the Ardbeg rinse and long, dry, herbal notes.

½ teaspoon Ardbeg 10 year Scotch whisky

1¾ oz. Glenmorangie the quinta ruban Scotch whisky

⅞ oz. plum sake

¼ oz. Noilly Prat dry vermouth

1 teaspoon Green Chartreuse

---

1. Rinse the goblet with the Ardbeg and discard any excess.

2. Place the remaining ingredients in a mixing glass, fill it two-thirds of the way with ice, and stir until chilled.

3. Strain into the goblet, garnish with dark chocolate or walnuts on the side, and enjoy.

GLASSWARE: Glencairn glass
GARNISH: Edible flowers

SHINTO DAISY

A whisky-based cocktail that a non-whisky drinker likely would enjoy, and it doubles as a gateway to other whisky-based drinks. It's refreshing, and also allows the primary spirit to shine without being overwhelming. It balances fruity, sweet, and sour flavors. Feel free to adjust the sweetness by adding more syrup.

1¼ oz. Mars Kasei whisky

⅞ oz. fresh lemon juice

⅞ oz. plum sake

1¾ teaspoons Demerara Syrup (see page 36)

8 dashes of Peychaud's bitters

3 dashes Ms. Better's bitters miraculous foamer or 1 egg white

---

1. Place all of the ingredients in a cocktail shaker and dry shake for 15 seconds.

2. Add ice to the shaker and shake vigorously until chilled.

3. Strain over two ice cubes into the Glencairn glass, garnish with the edible flowers, and enjoy.

TEQUILA & MEZCAL

For starters, all tequila is mezcal. But not all mezcal is tequila. Those of you who are confused, think of it this way: all bourbon is whiskey, but not all whiskey is bourbon.

Both tequila and mezcal are made by distilling the core of the agave plant, known as the piña. There are about 30 different varietals of agave plant that can be used to make mezcals.

Only blue agave can be used to produce tequila. Tequila and mezcal come from different regions of Mexico. Tequila makers can be found in the northern and central parts of the country—Michoacán, Guanajuato, Nayarit, Tamaulipas, and Jalisco, which is where the town of Tequila is located. Oaxaca, which is in southern Mexico, is where 85 percent of mezcal is produced, though it is also made in Durango, Guanajuato, Guerrero, San Luis Potosí, Tamaulipas, Zacatecas, Michoacán, and Puebla.

The separation between the two spirits, in the global imagination, began with Mexico's victory in 1810's War of Independence. Fueled by the energy of that unexpected triumph, those in charge of the burgeoning republic began to look to an increasingly industrialized Europe for inspiration. In Tequila, mezcal producers started to shake off the yoke of the hacienda system, gaining the ability to acquire more capital—resources they had the wisdom to reinvest into their operations. Eventually, Martin Martinez de Castro introduced the copper column still to the town. This innovation, when combined with the development of cooking the agave in a stone oven instead of the traditional earthen pit, bolstered production immensely.

From there, it was little more than a numbers game. Tequila, through sheer quantity and market share, became embedded in most people's minds as Mexico's spirit. And mezcal, by remaining tied to the craft culture that had fostered it, came—until very recently—to be seen as an altogether separate category, a curiosity surrounded by myth, and misunderstanding.

To make tequila, the agave is steamed in ovens before being distilled in copper stills.

Once distilled, it is aged in oak barrels, and the amount of time spent in the barrel determines the type of tequila that is bottled. A breakdown of the various types follows:

Plata (no more than 2 months): Also called blanco, silver, joven, or white tequila, this is the purest form of distilled blue agave. Once it has been distilled, it is quickly bottled and distributed. Plata should taste fresh and fruity, with a clean, herbaceous hint. If reposado or añejo tequila is not specified for use in the following cocktails, assume that plata should be used.

Reposado (2 to 12 months): Extra time in the barrel lets this "rested" tequila mellow out, and imparts a hint of flavors, ranging from oak to vanilla, baking spices, and fruit.

Añejo (1 to 3 years): This tequila has more depth and complexity than both plata and reposado, featuring notes of wood, nuts, and chocolate. While each brand is unique in terms of wood used and resting time, all añejo is going to be soft, smooth, and distinct on the palate.

Extra Añejo (minimum of 3 years): This "extra aged" variety is a relative newcomer to the scene, only becoming an official classification in March 2006.

Tequila, like Champagne, is a designated Appellation of Origin (AO). Like all mezcal, the agave used to produce tequila is tended to by individuals known as jimadors, who still largely perform their work by hand. In order to get a product that is saleable, these jimadors have to plant the agave, care for the plants, and harvest them when they are perfectly ripe. A huge amount of time, energy, and passion gets put into every bottle of pure blue agave tequila. That's even more the case when the tequila is aged.

If you've noticed the continual appearance of "pure" in reference to tequila, that is not an accident. Most everyone knows someone who has tequila firmly on their personal no-fly list.

This is undoubtedly due to an encounter with a tequila that was less than 100 percent blue agave, or a mixto. Since they are cheaper to produce, there are many more mixto brands on the market than there are pure agave brands.

Legally, these mixto tequilas must be made with at least 51 percent pure blue agave sugar. The other portion of the sugars can be from non-agave sources, like sugarcane, which will affect the taste of the spirit in a negative fashion, and potentially make the aftereffects of an evening much worse. So, in order to make sure you're getting the best experience, carefully read the label of any tequila bottle before you purchase, and say no to mixtos.

To produce mezcal, the agave is cooked over charcoal in basalt-lined pits dug in the ground and distillation happens in clay vessels; this is why most mezcals have a smoky flavor, though, as with Scotch, there are exceptions, with some offerings featuring no smoke at all, and others just a trace to provide balance. Like tequila, mezcal is aged in oak barrels.

Until recently, most people outside of Mexico marked mezcal as "the one with the worm." The existence of this meme appears to be tied to a popular marketing campaign put forth by the Monte Alban brand during the '70s. The worm, or gusano, appeared in every bottle of Monte Alban, but it is not a hallmark of the spirit, as many believed. Though it does still pop up from time to time. The gusano, which feeds upon the agave plant, is believed to be highly nutritious. It can be consumed on

its own, or dropped into a bottle, where it does everything from hide unpleasant flavors to add a subtle, pleasant fungal note to a well-crafted mezcal.

Mezcal, due to its association with the rural south of Mexico and the folk cultures that prevail there, was also misunderstood within Mexico for a long period of time. This began to change when a growing appreciation for craft and heritage entered the national mindset, shifting mezcal from an easily dismissed oddity to a powerfully deep tradition that shifts as one moves from village to village. This rich provincialism contributed much to the lore that surrounds mezcal, including the claim that it will cause those that imbibe to hallucinate. While that is not the case, there is a school that believes the agave sugars in mezcal do produce a stimulating and energizing effect that causes a slightly higher degree of awareness than that which is employed in everyday life.

When selecting a mezcal, much can be determined by looking at the percentage of alcohol. Simply put, the higher the ABV, the less watered down the product is, and the more oils the distillate will contain. These oils provide the spirit with rich flavors and complexity, which is appealing to the aficionado, less so to the entrepreneur looking for global appeal, as they are after a cleaner tasting product with less variance. A good rule of thumb: anything at 40 percent ABV is made for a foreign market, though some of these offerings are designated as single village, meaning they will carry a distinctive character. Anything at 46 percent and up can be trusted to carry the taste of a traditional mezcal.

For cocktails, it's certainly worth experimenting with any mezcal you enjoy, but Del Maguey's Vida offering is a good default option, since it was designed in response to bartenders asking the company to make something that was more amenable to crafting cocktails. Tropical, fruity, and toasty, Vida will to be prove a comfortable fit in a surprising number of situations, making it an ideal spirit to work with when using mezcal to improvise a riff on a classic, or construct something totally new.

HOME IS WHERE THE HEAT IS

A cocktail where each sip provides something new to consider, thanks in large part to the presence of the capricious flavor of tamarind.

Lava salt, for the rim

Cumin, for the rim

1½ oz. Spicy Mezcal (see recipe)

¼ oz. Giffard banane du brésil liqueur

½ oz. fresh lime juice

½ oz. Manzanilla sherry

¾ oz. Tamarind Syrup (see recipe)

---

1. Place lava salt and cumin in a dish and stir to combine. Wet the rim of the double rocks glass and coat it with the mixture.

2. Place the remaining ingredients in a cocktail shaker, fill it two-thirds of the way with ice, and shake vigorously until chilled.

3. Strain over ice into the rimmed glass, garnish with the dehydrated slice of jalapeño, and enjoy

SPICY MEZCAL: Place sliced jalapeño in a bottle of mezcal and let it steep for 24 hours—determine the amount of jalapeños and the length of time you steep the mixture based on your spice tolerance. Strain before using or storing, and reserve the leftover jalapeños to garnish other cocktails or serve as a boozy and yummy snack.

TAMARIND SYRUP: Place ¼ cup tamarind pulp, 1 cup water, and 1 cup sugar in a saucepan and bring to a simmer, stirring to dissolve the sugar and incorporate the tamarind. Remove the pan from heat and let the mixture cool completely. Strain before using or storing.

GARNISH: Watermelon slice, fresh cilantro

EL VATO SWIZZLE

An elevated Margarita that can be fashioned with the fruits
of a backyard garden.

½ oz. Olmeca Altos tequila

 oz. fresh lime juice

¼ oz. fresh watermelon juice

¼ oz. Mexican Pepper Reduction (see recipe)

Dash of Peychaud's Bitters

. Fill the pilsner glass with crushed ice and add the ingredients, except for the bitters, in the order they are listed.

. Use the swizzle method to combine: place a swizzle stick
between your hands, lower the swizzle stick into the drink,
and quickly rub your palms together to rotate the stick as
you move it up and down in the drink. When frost begins
to form on the outside of the glass, the drink is mixed.

. Top with the bitters and more crushed ice, garnish with

MEXICAN PEPPER REDUCTION: You
want to do this in a well-ventilated kitche
as the fumes from cooking the reduction
will make the air noxious. Place 4½ quart.
water, 10 dried chile de árbol peppers, 10
ancho chile peppers, and 6 jalapeño chile
peppers (sliced lengthwise, 4 with seeds,
2 without) in a large saucepan, bring to a
boil, and cook for 20 minutes. Strain into
large container. Due to evaporation durir
the boiling process, approximately half
a quart of liquid will have been lost. Add
water until you have 4 quarts of liquid. Ac
6 quarts sugar and stir until the sugar has
dissolved. Let the reduction cool complete
ly before using or storing in the refrigerator.

GLASSWARE: Quido Jakobsen Glass or rocks glass

GARNISH: Carrot & Habanero Powder (see recipe), edible flower

DESERT DAISY

A stunning tequila cocktail that does not need a gorgeous handmade glass in order to wow someone, but is so imaginative and well executed that it deserves such trappings.

1½ oz. Olmeca Altos tequila

½ oz. BroVo amaro #4

¾ oz. fresh lime juice

¾ oz. Bell Pepper & Beet Syrup (see recipe)

4 drops of 25 Percent Saline Solution (see recipe)

10 dashes of Bittermens hellfire habanero shrub

---

1. Place all of the ingredients in a cocktail shaker, fill it two-thirds of the way with ice, and shake vigorously until chilled.

2. Strain over ice into the chosen glass, and garnish with the Carrot & Habanero Powder and edible flower, and enjoy.

BELL PEPPER & BEET SYRUP: Juice ½ cup chopped orange bell pepper and ½ cup chopped beets separately and strain to remove any remaining pulp. Place the juices in a saucepan, add 1 cup sugar, and bring to a boil. Reduce heat so that the mixture simmers and stir until the sugar has dissolved. Remove the pan from heat and let the syrup cool completely before using or storing.

25 PERCENT SALINE SOLUTION: Place 1 oz. of salt in a measuring cup. Add warm water until you reach 4 oz. and the salt has dissolved. Let the solution cool before using or storing.

CARROT & HABANERO POWDER: Use a mortar and pestle to grind 2 tablespoons dehydrated carrots, 2 tablespoons red pepper flakes, and 2 tablespoons kosher salt into a fine powder.

LA DIOSA

The Pineapple Marmalade is far more complex than it seems on its face, and as such is an ingredient you will be continually searching for other places to incorporate it.

1½ oz. tequila

¾ oz. triple sec

½ oz. fresh lime juice

1 tablespoon Pineapple Marmalade (see recipe)

½ teaspoon red pepper flakes

1 small bunch of fresh cilantro

1 egg white

---

1. Place all of the ingredients, except for the egg white, in a cocktail shaker, fill it two-thirds of the way with ice, and shake until chilled.

2. Strain the cocktail, remove the ice from the shaker, and place the cocktail back in the shaker. Add egg white and shake vigorously for 10 seconds.

3. Strain the cocktail into the coupe, garnish with the edible flowers and House Tajín, and enjoy.

PINEAPPLE MARMALADE: Place the chopped flesh of 4 pineapples, 8 cinnamon sticks, ¼ cup pure vanilla extract, 4 orange peels, 2 deseeded dried guajillo chile peppers, 1 cup sweet vermouth, 1 cup Lillet, and 4 cups sugar in a saucepan and simmer gently until the liquid has reduced by at least half, 4 to 5 hours. Remove the cinnamon sticks and chiles, place the marmalade in a blender, and puree until smooth. Let the marmalade cool before using or storing.

HOUSE TAJÍN: Place 1 cup mesquite seasoning, 1 cup smoked paprika, ½ cup kosher salt, and the zest of 2 grapefruits in a container and stir to combine. Use as desired.

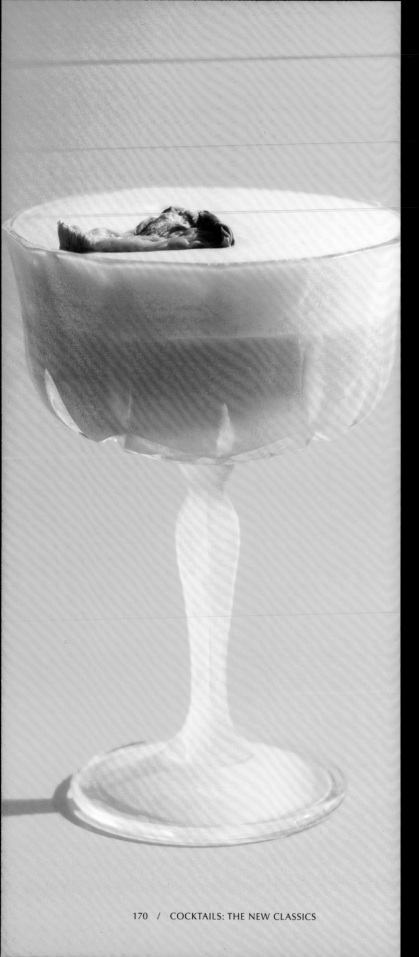

GLASS OFF

Inspired by the epic deep-cut from Bernie Leadon—best known as one of the founding members of The Eagles—th cocktail will whisk you away to some charming remove.

---

1 oz. mezcal

¾ oz. Aperol

⅞ oz. fresh lime juice

½ oz. Demerara Syrup (see page 36)

1¼ oz. pineapple juice

3 dashes of absinthe

1 egg white

---

1. Place all of the ingredients in a cocktail shaker contair no ice and dry shake for 15 seconds.

2. Fill the shaker two-thirds of the way with ice and shake vigorously until chilled.

3. Double strain the cocktail into the large coupe, garnis with the dehydrated pineapple slice, and enjoy.

MOLE YETI

A hint of mole's smoke and spice and a chocolate stout set the stage for a wondrously complex drink.

---

1 oz. añejo tequila

¾ oz. Leopold Bros. three pins alpine herbal liqueur

½ teaspoon chipotle chile powder

6 oz. chocolate stout

---

1. Place the tequila and liqueur in a mixing glass, fill it two-thirds of the way with ice, and stir until chilled.

2. Strain into a clean mixing glass, add the chipotle chile powder, and stir vigorously to completely incorporate it.

3. Strain into the goblet, slowly pour in the beer, and enjoy.

VIOLET SKIES

Bartenders across the world have fallen in love with the
togenic purple hue butterfly pea flower provides a cock

¾ oz. Butterfly Pea Flower–Infused Mezcal (see recipe)

½ oz. Hood River Distillers Lewis & Clark lookout gin

½ oz. Ventura Spirits strawberry brandy

¼ oz. Kalani coconut liqueur

¼ oz. Rothman & Winter crème de violette

½ oz. fresh lemon juice

2 dashes of Scrappy's grapefruit bitters

---

1. Chill the coupe in the freezer.

2. Place all of the ingredients in a cocktail shaker and d
   shake. Add ice and shake vigorously until chilled.

3. Double strain into the chilled coupe, garnish with an
   edible flower, and enjoy.

BUTTERFLY PEA FLOWER–INFUSED MEZCAL: Place 2
tablespoons dried butterfly pea flowers and a 750 ml bo
of mezcal in a mason jar, shake vigorously, and steep fo
hours. Strain before using or storing.

GLASSWARE: Coupe

GARNISH: None

NAKED & FAMOUS

The salmon pink color is a bit deceptive, as the drink is smoky thanks to the mezcal and bittersweet thanks to the Aperol. Another massive hit from the folks at New York's Death & Co.

¾ oz. mezcal

¾ oz. Yellow Chartreuse

¾ oz. Aperol

¾ oz. fresh lime juice

1. Chill the coupe in the freezer.

2. Place all of the ingredients in a cocktail shaker, fill it two-thirds of the way with ice, and shake vigorously until chilled.

3. Strain into the chilled coupe and enjoy.

HABITUAL LINE STEPPER

Pumpkin, tequila, the oxidative notes of brandy, and sherry yield a fascinating, toasty flavor profile that evokes the sweater wearing, leaves-on-the-ground sensation of a November day.

---

1 oz. Pumpkin Oil–Washed Tequila (see recipe)

¾ oz. Alma de Trabanco quinquina

⅓ oz. Glasshouse trade winds brandy

½ oz. Karabakh apricot brandy

½ oz. Grant Amontillado sherry

2 dashes of Bittercube Bolivar bitters

---

1. Place all of the ingredients in a mixing glass, fill it two-thirds of the way with ice, and stir until chilled.

2. Strain into the Nick & Nora glass, garnish with the fresh cilantro leaf, and enjoy.

PUMPKIN OIL–WASHED TEQUILA: Place a 750 ml bottle Partida reposado tequila and 3 tablespoons La Tourange toasted pumpkin seed oil in a large mason jar. Seal and store it in a dark, cool spot for 5 days. After 5 days, place the jar in the freezer and leave it until the oil has congeale about 12 hours. Strain the mixture through a coffee filter remove all the oil from the tequila. If there are globules o left, refreeze and strain again until the tequila is complete free of oil.

RISING SUN

The rare cocktail that doesn't improve when fresh fruit juice is switched in for the stuff in a bottle.

Salt, for the rim

1 maraschino cherry

1½ oz. tequila

⅔ oz. Yellow Chartreuse

½ oz. Rose's lime cordial

1 bar spoon sloe gin

---

1. Wet the rim of the coupe and coat with the salt. Place the cherry in the bottom of the glass and set the rimmed glass aside.

2. Place the tequila, Chartreuse, and cordial in a cocktail shaker, fill it two-thirds of the way with ice, and shake vigorously until chilled.

3. Strain into the rimmed glass, top with the sloe gin, let it filter down through the cocktail, and enjoy.

MUCHO ALOHA

Vida mezcal, the blended version Del Maguey offered in response to bartenders around the world demanding a mezcal
intended for use in cocktails, forms the base of this unique
clarified milk punch.

---

2 oz. Del Maguey vida mezcal

½ oz. Plantation pineapple rum

1 oz. fresh lemon juice

1 oz. Spiced Pineapple Syrup (see recipe)

½ oz. Simple Syrup (see page 26)

3 dashes of cinnamon bitters

Raw whole milk, as needed

---

1. Place all of the ingredients, except for the milk, in a bowl
    and stir until well combined.

2. Add about 1 oz. milk and allow it to curdle. To turn this
    into a punch, maintain the ratios, adding about 20 per-
    cent milk to the amount of the liquids mezcal, rum, lemon
    juice, and syrups, as well as water for desired dilution.

3. Store the mixture in the refrigerator for 24 hours.

4. Strain the mixture through cheesecloth until a clear, shiny
    liquid is achieved. Serve over ice in rocks glasses.

SPICED PINEAPPLE SYRUP: Place 1 part Pineapple Juice
(see recipe) and 1 part Spiced Pineapple Water (see recipe)
in a mason jar and stir to combine.

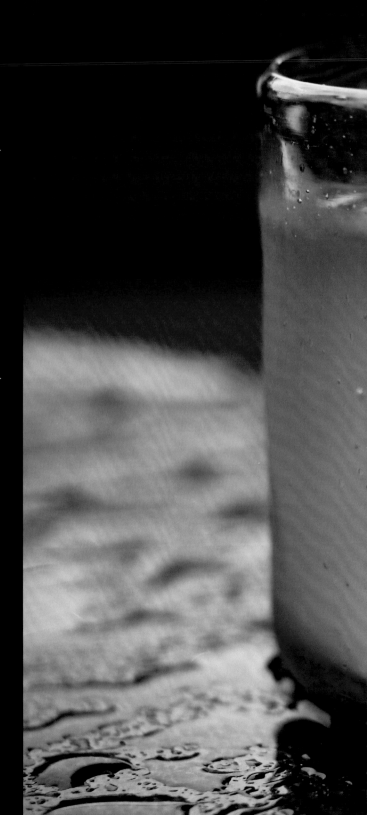

PINEAPPLE JUICE: Remove the skin and core from a fresh pineapple, reserving both for the Spiced Pineapple Water. Chop the pineapple flesh, place it in a blender, and puree until smooth. Strain through a chinois.

SPICED PINEAPPLE WATER: Place the reserved pineapple skin and core, cinnamon sticks, a chipotle chile pepper, allspice berries, whole cloves, cacao nibs, and 6 quarts water in a sauce pan and warm over low heat. Cook until the water is very fragrant. Strain before using or storing in the refrigerator.

GLASSWARE: Tiki mug

GARNISH: Luxardo maraschino cherry, pineapple wedge, edible orchid, pineapple leaves

HISTORIA DE UN AMOR

One for those who find themselves torn between their loves for agave spirits and tiki.

1½ oz. tequila

½ oz. mezcal

¾ oz. fresh lime juice

¾ oz. Pineapple Syrup (see recipe)

¼ oz. Passion Fruit Syrup (see page 59)

5 dashes of Thai Chile Tincture (see recipe)

---

1. Place all of the ingredients in a cocktail shaker, add 2 or 3 ice cubes, and shake vigorously until chilled. This method of mixing is known as a whip shake.

2. Fill the tiki mug with crushed ice and strain the cocktail over it.

3. Garnish the cocktail with the maraschino cherry, pineapple wedge, edible orchid, and pineapple leaves and enjoy.

PINEAPPLE SYRUP: Place 1 pineapple that has been trimmed and cut into cubes and 4 cups sugar in a large container and let the pineapple macerate for 4 hours. Place the mixture in a blender and puree until smooth. Strain the syrup before using or storing.

THAI CHILE TINCTURE: Place 4 chopped bird's eye chile peppers and a 750 ml bottle of Wray & Nephew rum in a large mason jar and steep for 2 weeks. Strain the tincture before using or storing.

PAMPLEMOUSSE AU POIVRE

A perfect balance of smoke, spice, and tanginess that took San Francisco by storm following its appearance in 2018.

---

2 oz. mezcal

1 oz. Giffard crème de pamplemousse liqueur

½ oz. Elixir de Poivre Cordial (see recipe)

½ oz. fresh lemon juice

Dash of Bitter Truth Grapefruit Bitters

---

1. Place all of the ingredients in a cocktail shaker, fill it two-thirds of the way with ice, and shake vigorously until chilled.

2. Strain into the tumbler, either over crushed ice and garnished with a sprinkle of pink peppercorns and a wide lemon twist, or up into a cocktail glass and garnished with a grapefruit peel cone filled with pink peppercorns rested on the rim.

ELIXIR DE POIVRE CORDIAL: Place 1 cup Stolen Heart vodka (120 proof), 1 tablespoon pink peppercorns, ¼ teaspoon Sichuan peppercorns, and ½ teaspoon coriander seeds in a mason jar, cover, and let the mixture sit at room temperature for 24 hours. Strain and then mix with Simple Syrup (see page 26) at a 1:1 ratio.

THE SAINT-GERMAIN

An elegant cocktail that is accessible at the same time.

½ oz. tequila

¾ oz. Yellow Chartreuse

½ oz. Pineapple Syrup (see page 179)

oz. fresh lime juice

fresh sage leaves

Place all of the ingredients in a cocktail shaker, fill it two-thirds of the way with ice, and shake vigorously until chilled.

Fill the tumbler with pebble ice and strain the cocktail over it.

Garnish with lime zest and enjoy.

Khus, a fragrant herb with a subtle sandalwood aroma, keys the unique flavors in this cocktail.

---

2 oz. tequila

1 oz. fresh lime juice

¾ oz. Spicy Cilantro & Khus Syrup (see recipe)

Coconut Foam (see recipe), for topping

---

1. Place the tequila, lime juice, and syrup in a cocktail shaker, fill it two-thirds of the way with ice, and shake vigorously until chilled.

2. Double strain into the coupe, top with the Coconut Foam, and garnish with the orange blossom.

SPICY CILANTRO & KHUS SYRUP: Place 4 cups khus syrup (available online or in specialty grocery stores), 1 bunch of fresh cilantro, and 5 Thai chile peppers in a blender and puree until smooth. Strain before using or storing.

COCONUT FOAM: Place 10 oz. coconut milk, 5 oz. Simple Syrup (see page 26), 10 oz. egg whites, 10 drops of coconut extract, and ½ oz. saline in an ISI whipping double charge with NO2 and shake well before dispensing.

PEACH TEA

A perfect summertime thirst-quencher, that can easily be batched to refresh a large crew.

½ oz. Silver Needle–Infused Tequila (see recipe)

½ oz. Ocho Blanco tequila

¾ oz. Peach Cordial (see recipe)

Drop of clary sage tincture

Dash of Merlet crème de pêche

Club soda, to top

---

1. Place all of the ingredients, except for the club soda, in a highball glass, add ice, and stir until chilled.

2. Top with club soda, garnish with the lemon wedge, and enjoy.

SILVER NEEDLE–INFUSED TEQUILA: Place 10½ oz. Ocho Blanco tequila and ⅛ oz. loose-leaf silver needle tea in a mason jar and steep for 24 hours. Strain before using or storing.

PEACH CORDIAL: Pit 4½ lbs. of peaches and puree the peaches. Stir 2 teaspoons of Pectinex Ultra SP-L into the puree and then spin the mixture in a centrifuge at 4200 rpm for 20 minutes. Strain the resulting juice through a coffee filter. Add 53 oz. caster (superfine) sugar and 1 oz. citric acid to the juice and stir until the sugar has dissolved. Stir in 10 drops of galbanum tincture and use immediately or store in the refrigerator.

GLASSWARE: Rocks glass

GARNISH: Orange wedge

MR. KOTTER

A combo of the classic Margarita, which has orange liqueur, and the new age version, which has agave nectar. By including a Hibiscus Ice Cube (see recipe) to add tartness, you can take advantage of both.

---

2 oz. Tapatio tequila

½ oz. Pierre Ferrand curaçao

1 oz. fresh lime juice

¼ oz. agave nectar

---

1. Place all of the ingredients in a cocktail shaker, fill it two-thirds of the way with ice, and shake vigorously until chilled.

2. Double strain over a Hibiscus Ice Cube into the rocks glass, garnish with an orange wedge, and enjoy.

HIBISCUS ICE CUBES: Place 8 cups water, 1 cup hibiscus blossoms, and an entire orange peel in a saucepan and bring to a boil. Remove the pan from heat and let the mixture steep for 3 hours. Strain, pour the strained liquid into ice molds, and freeze.

A Paloma is refreshing in its own right. Add some bubbles to the proceedings, and it becomes an outright oasis.

¾ oz. tequila

1¼ oz. ruby red grapefruit juice

1¼ oz. white grapefruit juice

Dash of Cinnamon Syrup (see page 127)

Champagne, to top

---

1. Place all of the ingredients, except for the Champagne, in the champagne flute and stir to combine.

2. Top with Champagne, garnish with the grapefruit twist, and enjoy.

LET'S FALL IN LOVE TONIGHT

A drink that evokes those rare times when everything comes together. For the tequila blend, Olmeca Altos, Ocho Blanco, and Fortaleza reposado are strongly recommended.

1¾ oz. tequila blend

¾ oz. fresh lemon juice

⅞ oz. Honey Water (see recipe)

---

1. Place all of the ingredients in a cocktail shaker, fill it two-thirds of the way with ice, and shake vigorously until chilled.

2. Double strain over ice into the rocks glass, garnish with the sprig of fresh lemon thyme, and enjoy.

HONEY WATER: Place 1 cup wildflower honey and 1 cup warm water in a mason jar, stir to combine, and let the mixture cool completely before using or storing.

GLASSWARE: Collins glass

GARNISH: Grapefruit wheel, lime wheel, dehydrated grapefruit chip

GUERA

The partnership of tequila and grapefruit is so successful that it can withstand any amount of heat—even that provided by the potent Thai Pepper Syrup.

1½ oz. tequila

1 oz. grapefruit juice

¾ oz. fresh lime juice

¼ oz. Aperol

¼ oz. St-Germain

¼ oz. Thai Pepper Shrub (see recipe)

Fever-Tree bitter lemon soda, to top

1. Place all of the ingredients, except for the soda, in a Collins glass, add ice, and stir until chilled.

2. Top with soda, garnish with the grapefruit wheel, lime wheel, and dehydrated grapefruit chip.

THAI PEPPER SHRUB: Place 4 chopped Thai chile peppers, ¼ cup cane vinegar, and ¼ cup cane sugar in a saucepan and bring to a boil. Cook for 5 minutes, remove the pan from heat, and let the shrub cool completely. Strain before using or storing.

GLASSWARE: Rocks glass

GARNISH: Sprig of pink pepper

TOMATO BEEF

As enjoyable as a pristine plate of caprese salad consumed on a veranda in August.

1¼ oz. tequila

¼ oz. basil eau de vie

1 oz. Tomato Water (see recipe)

½ oz. Pink Peppercorn Syrup (see recipe)

½ oz. fresh lime juice

---

1. Place all of the ingredients in a mixing glass, fill it two-thirds of the way with ice, and stir until chilled.

2. Strain over ice into the rocks glass, garnish with the sprig of pink pepper, and enjoy.

TOMATO WATER: Place tomatoes in a blender, puree until smooth, and strain through a coffee filter.

PINK PEPPERCORN SYRUP: Place 3 cups sugar and 2 cups water in a saucepan and bring to a simmer, stirring to dissolve the sugar. Add 2 tablespoons pink peppercorns or 10 pink pepper sprigs to the syrup, simmer for 20 minutes, and strain. Let the syrup cool completely before using or storing.

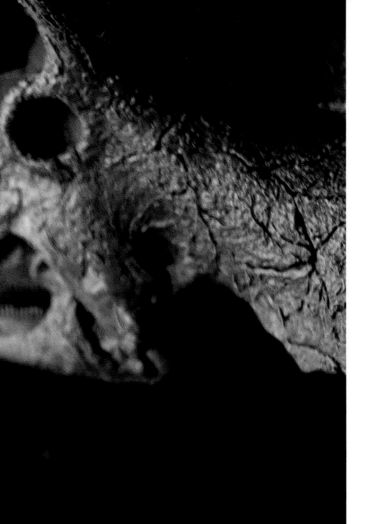

GLASSWARE: Ceramic bowl

GARNISH: Cornflower leaves

HAY ZEUS

A cocktail that hones in on the grassy, green, and vegetal vibes you get from highland tequila and mezcals.

½ oz. Olmeca Altos tequila

½ oz. fresh lime juice

1¾ oz. Zeus Juice Cordial (see recipe)

---

1. Place all of the ingredients in a cocktail shaker, fill it two-thirds of the way with ice, and shake vigorously until chilled.

2. Place a large ice cube in the ceramic bowl and strain the cocktail over it.

3. Garnish with the cornflower leaves and enjoy.

ZEUS JUICE CORDIAL: Place ⅜ oz. crushed hay, 5¼ oz. celery juice, and 3½ oz. caster (superfine) sugar in a blender and puree until smooth. Strain the mixture through cheesecloth and stir in ⅞ oz. Simple Syrup (see page 26), 1 cup mezcal, 3½ oz. blue wine (Gik is a trusted brand), ½ oz. 5 percent Saline Solution (see page 73), and 2 drops of MSK Toasted Coconut Flavour Drops. Use immediately or store in the refrigerator.

TIA MIA

Adding just a little smoke to the Mai Tai provides a far more thoughtful experience.

---

1 oz. mezcal

1 oz. aged Jamaican rum

¾ oz. fresh lime juice

½ oz. Orgeat (see page 57)

½ oz. Pierre Ferrand curaçao

---

1. Place all of the ingredients in a cocktail shaker, fill it two-thirds of the way with ice, and shake vigorously until chilled.

2. Fill the rocks glass with crushed ice and strain the cocktail over it.

3. Garnish with the fresh mint, lime wheel, and edible orchid and enjoy.

GUN METAL BLUE

The flaming garnish suits a cocktail that is both eye-catching and worthy of contemplation.

1½ oz. mezcal

½ oz. blue curaçao

¼ oz. peach brandy

¾ oz. fresh lime juice

¼ oz. Cinnamon Syrup (see page 127)

---

1. Chill the coupe in the freezer.

2. Place all of the ingredients in a cocktail shaker, fill it two-thirds of the way with ice, and shake vigorously until chilled.

3. Strain into the coupe. Place the orange peel skin side down on top of the drink, taking care not to wet the top side.

4. Gently fill coin with a couple of drops of overproof rum and carefully ignite it. Enjoy, carefully.

THIRD PLAYER

A cocktail that runs in a number of directions, yet is still comforting and accessible, thanks to the sense of campfire elicited by the smoke and warming spices.

¾ oz. mezcal

½ oz. cachaça

½ oz. Toasted Black Cardamom & Cinnamon Maple Syrup (see recipe)

½ oz. fresh lime juice

¼ oz. pisco

¼ oz. apricot liqueur

¼ oz. Ancho Reyes

½ oz. Orgeat (see page 57)

¼ oz. falernum

2 dashes of Bittermens xocolatl mole bitters

Pinch of salt

TOASTED BLACK CARDAMOM & CINNAMON MAPLE SYRUP:
Place 2 cinnamon sticks and 3 black cardamom pods in a skillet and toast over medium heat until fragrant, shaking the pan frequently. Remove the aromatics from the pan and set them aside. Place 1 cup maple syrup and ½ cup water in a saucepan and bring to a simmer. Add the toasted spices and simmer for 5 minutes. Remove the pan from heat and let the mixture cool for 1 hour. Strain before using or storing.

1. Place all of the ingredients in a cocktail shaker, fill it two-thirds of the way with ice, and shake vigorously until chilled.

2. Fill the rocks glass with crushed ice and strain the cocktail over it.

3. Garnish with crushed cinnamon sticks and enjoy.

CANOE CLUB

The jammy and tart flavor of crème de mure keeps the significant spice added by the syrup from running away with this cocktail.

1½ oz. mezcal

½ oz. crème de mûre

¾ oz. Ginger & Serrano Syrup (see recipe)

½ oz. fresh lime juice

3 dashes of Peychaud's bitters

---

1. Place all of the ingredients in a cocktail shaker, stir to combine, fill the shaker two-thirds of the way with ice, and shake vigorously until chilled.

2. Fill the rocks glass with crushed or pebble ice, strain the cocktail over it, and enjoy.

GINGER & SERRANO SYRUP: Place 2 cups sugar, 1 cup water, 3 chopped serrano chile peppers, and 2 large chopped pieces of ginger in a saucepan and bring to a simmer, stirring to dissolve the sugar. Cook for 10 minutes and strain the syrup into a mason jar. Let the syrup cool completely before using or storing.

GLASSWARE: Clay cup

GARNISH: Pineapple leaves, lime wheel, marigold blossom

FLOR DE JALISCO

The rustic air provided by the clay cup belies the refined and complex cocktail that lies within.

1½ oz. Altos Olmeca reposado tequila

½ oz. Del Maguey vida mezcal

½ oz. strawberry jam

½ oz. agave nectar

½ oz. fresh lime juice

Dash of Black Lava Solution (see recipe)

3 dashes of Bittermens hellfire habanero shrub

---

1. Place all of the ingredients in a cocktail shaker, fill it two-thirds of the way with ice, and shake vigorously until chilled.

2. Strain over ice into the clay cup, garnish with the pineapple leaves, lime wheel, and marigold blossom, and enjoy.

BLACK LAVA SOLUTION: Place ½ cup water and ¼ cup black lava salt in a saucepan and bring to a boil. Remove the pan from heat and stir to dissolve the salt. Let the solution cool completely before using or storing.

PICA FRESA

Smooth and refreshing, with just enough spice to hold your attention.

1½ oz. tequila

½ oz. fresh lemon juice

½ oz. Cucumber Syrup (see recipe)

½ oz. Pickled Strawberry & Fresno Chile Brine (see recipe)

---

1. Chill the coupe in the refrigerator.

2. Place all of the ingredients in a cocktail shaker, fill it two-thirds of the way with ice, and shake vigorously until chilled.

3. Strain into the chilled coupe, garnish with a dusting of chipotle chile powder, and enjoy.

CUCUMBER SYRUP: Place 1 cup freshly pressed cucumber juice and 1 cup caster (superfine) sugar in a blender and puree until the sugar has dissolved. Use immediately or store in the refrigerator.

PICKLED STRAWBERRY & FRESNO CHILE BRINE: Place 1 cup white balsamic vinegar, 1 cup water, 1 teaspoon salt, and ¼ cup sugar in a saucepan and bring to a boil, stirring to dissolve the sugar. Place 10 hulled and quartered straw-berries and 2 deseeded, sliced Fresno chiles in a heatproof container. Pour the brine over the strawberries and chiles and let the mixture cool to room temperature. Strain before using or storing in the refrigerator.

GLASSWARE: Emptied pineapple shell

GARNISH: Pineapple leaves, orange slices, fresh mint, Tajín, cocktail umbrella

DRUNKEN RABBIT

Featuring notes of caramel, chocolate, and vanilla, Ancho Reyes carries a depth that is uncommon in spicy spirits.

2 oz. mezcal

1 oz. Ancho Reyes

1½ oz. pineapple juice

1½ oz. guava juice

1 oz. Cinnamon Syrup (see page 127)

1. Place all of the ingredients in a blender, add 2 oz. crushed ice, and puree until smooth.

2. Pour the cocktail into the pineapple shell, garnish with the pineapple leaves, orange slices, fresh mint, Tajín, and cocktail umbrella, and enjoy.

GLASSWARE: Clay cup

GARNISH: Fresh mint, cinnamon stick

SHAKE YOUR TAMARIND

The tamarind brings some tangy notes that highlight the blend of tequila and mezcal.

1½ oz. reposado tequila

¼ oz. mezcal

¼ oz. Campari

¾ oz. tamarind concentrate

¾ oz. Cinnamon Syrup (see page 127)

¼ oz. fresh lime juice

---

1. Place all of the ingredients in a mixing glass, fill it two-thirds of the way with ice, and stir until chilled.

2. Double strain into the clay cup, garnish with the fresh mint and cinnamon stick, and enjoy.

GLASSWARE: Goblet

GARNISH: Strip of orange peel

UNSCALPE

Resting Kamm & Sons' famed British aperitif in a cask that used to hold a peated Islay Scotch resulted in a limited edition bottling that excited bartenders around the world—and this elegant cocktail.

1½ oz. mezcal

1 oz. Kamm & Sons Islay cask

1 oz. Aperol

1. Place all of the ingredients in a mixing glass, fill it two-thirds of the way with ice, and stir until chilled.

2. Strain into a goblet, garnish with the strip of orange peel, and enjoy.

OAXACA OLD FASHIONED

Created by agave spirits evangelist Phil Ward at the infamous Death & Co., this is the cocktail that got the cocktail world excited about mezcal. Don't be afraid to experiment with the type of bitters employed in this one—in an evolved version Ward went with Bittermens Xocalatl mole bitters—or to go all-in on a mezcal-only version.

1½ oz. reposado tequila

½ oz. mezcal

2 dashes of Angostura bitters

1 bar spoon agave nectar

---

1. Place a large ice cube in the rocks glass. Add all of the ingredients and stir until chilled.

2. Hold the strip of orange peel about 2 inches above a lit match for a couple of seconds. Twist and squeeze the peel over the lit match, while holding it above the cocktail and taking care to avoid the flames.

3. Rub the torched peel around the rim of the glass, drop it into the drink, and enjoy.

GLASSWARE: Cocktail glass

GARNISH: Pineapple leaf, lemon wedge

PIÑA FUMADA

Any mezcal will work in this drink, but Quiquiriqui, with its peppery finish, is the best option to counter all the spice and sweetness.

1¼ oz. mezcal

¾ oz. fresh lemon juice

2 teaspoons falernum

½ oz. honey

Club soda, to top

---

1. Place all of the ingredients, except for the club soda, in a cocktail shaker, fill it two-thirds of the way with ice, and shake vigorously until chilled.

2. Fill the Collins glass with crushed ice and strain the cocktail over it.

3. Top the cocktail with club soda and more crushed ice.

4. Garnish with the pineapple leaf and lemon wedge and enjoy.

DIABLO OTOÑO

A light but surprisingly complex drink, thanks to the Fig Cordial and the slightly bitter note added by the tonic.

---

oz. tequila

oz. Fig Cordial (see recipe)

teaspoon fig liqueur

Tonic water, to top

---

1. Place three ice spheres in the Collins glass. Add all of the ingredients, except for the tonic water, and stir until chilled.

2. Top with the tonic water and enjoy.

FIG CORDIAL: Preheat the oven to 350°F. Place 15 quartered figs on a parchment-lined baking sheet, drizzle 3½ oz. honey over them, and then sprinkle 1¾ oz. walnuts around the pan. Place the pan in the oven and bake for 10 minutes. While the figs and walnuts are in the oven, place the Fig Leaf Syrup (see recipe) in a saucepan and warm it over medium heat. When the figs and walnuts are done, remove them from the oven, add them to the syrup, and simmer for 10 minutes. Strain the mixture into a mason jar, stir in 1 tablespoon citric acid and 7 oz. Rosé, and let the cordial cool completely before using or storing.

FIG LEAF SYRUP: Place 30 fig leaves in a container and pour 3 cups of warm Simple Syrup (see page 26) over them. Steep for 30 minutes and strain before using or storing.

As it is easily the most diverse spirit on Earth, the process of working with rum while making cocktails is a fun one. But it also can be overwhelming, with offerings from more than 60 countries available to sample.

To start, rum is known for its sweetness, and, considering that it is made by distilling sugarcane or sugarcane byproducts, there's no getting away from this aspect of its flavor profile. The industry rose from the sticky dregs of colonialism, which flourished in the Caribbean thanks to the free labor provided by slavery. Rum is the result of yeast being added to the molasses that is a byproduct of boiling the juice from harvested sugarcane.

This "wash" is then allowed to ferment for anywhere from 24 hours to 2 weeks, and then distilled. The fermentation process affects rum's flavor in two ways. The length of the fermentation period will have considerable impact, with more aromatic and flavorful substances developing the longer the fermentation is allowed to proceed. The second major influence is the type of yeast used. Many distillers have developed their own distinct strains over the years and are highly protective of them—in fact, Bacardí is so concerned about the possible corruption of the yeast used to power their global empire that they store some of the original in a climate-controlled vault in Switzerland. A few Jamaican producers utilize a method similar to the sourdough starter that has become all the rage in bread baking. Kept in "dunder pits," wood-lined pits hidden in the ground, these wild yeasts are fed by leftover wash, eventually producing the funk Jamaican rums are known and loved for.

Once the wash is made, it has to be distilled to produce rum. The pot still is the oldest of the methods used to distill rum, and it is essentially a large kettle where the wash is brought to a boil, with any vapors condensed and collected.

Another pass through the pot still will then bring the spirit to proof, and then the rum will be rested in stainless steel tanks or oak barrels so that the bold flavors present when the rum comes out of the still can mellow. For centuries, the pot still was the only option available to distillers, but with the Industrial Revolution came the advent of the column still, an innovation that proved to be a huge leap forward in terms of production and efficiency. A column still requires less wash and less energy to produce spirits, and it also can be fed continuously with wash, as opposed to the batches which must be added and then removed from the pot still. Another advantage of the column still is the higher-proof and lighter-bodied spirit it produces, a style that has a much broader appeal. But, for all of those advantages, the column still cannot touch the pot in terms of creating the various aromas and flavors that appeal to the craftsman and the connoisseur. To solve this problem, rum producers have followed in the footsteps of the Scottish, who have been using a combination of pot and column distillates to create blended Scotch whisky since the nineteenth century. Grabbing the best of both approaches, the spirits are then blended and aged or aged separately before being combined, resulting in rums that are smoother on the palate and more complex, despite not being aged for as long as they typically would have to be to achieve these measures.

People assume that any clear rum has not been aged, but that is not the case for all but a few products on the market. In most white or clear rums, the color has been removed via charcoal filtration. This misapprehension regarding clear rums also feeds the belief that all of the golden-hued rums on the shelf get that color from the barrel. That may well be the case, but a rum's color can also come from a distiller adding caramel coloring, a practice used to trick the uninitiated into thinking complexity and depth will be there, when in reality they aren't. As for black rums, they are typically unaged or very briefly aged blended rums that receive their dark shade from the addition of caramel and/or molasses. In this category, a consideration of color is actually helpful, because it defines the category.

In light of the complications that can result from using color as a guide, some will rely on the age statement featured on the spirit's label. But this can also imply a wide range of possibilities. In some countries, like Barbados, Jamaica, and Guyana, the age statement will be the youngest rum featured in the blend. In other countries, such as those which use the solera-style method of aging, the age statement will reflect the oldest spirit present. And, on occasion, the rum will forgo a precise mention of age and employ terms that imply extended stints in a barrel, like añejo or XO, but are not guided by any strict guidelines.

Blended rums that have been lightly aged (1 to 4 years), such as Appleton Estate's funky reserve blend, or El Dorado's 3 Year offering, are good go-to's for the majority of the cocktails in this book, and rums in this age range have been rested long enough to let the nature of the spirit come through, but not long enough to take on too much influence from the barrel, beyond color. But there are more than a few instances where a more mature rum, aged from 5 to 14 years, is called for. For those familiar with the higher price tags that extended aging can come with, rest assured—these aged rums, which are also wonderful for sipping neat, carry a much lower price tag than similarly aged Scotches or bourbons. For the devotee of blended rums, Venezuela's Diplomático and El Dorado are the best aged options, while Ron Zacapa 23 and Flor de Caña are wonderful options produced via the column still.

In your travels through the world of rum, you will also come across rhum agricole and cachaça. The former is made from sugarcane juice instead of molasses, and, since it is not fermented before being distilled, it tends to by drier and more vegetal than its close cousin. Cachaça is often referred to as "Brazilian rum," as it is the South American nation's preferred spirit. Like rum, it is fermented, but, as with rhum agricole, sugarcane juice is the raw material. This results in a grassier, rawer spirit that is more inclined to being affected by elements like terroir and the type of wood used to age it than other rums.

Of course, any trip to the rum section at a liquor store is going to meet with a numbered of flavored rums. In short, the serious practitioner should avoid them at all costs, and take matters into their own hands, whether it be making their own Spiced Rum (see page 240), or simply incorporating the flavor they want—coconut, mango, passion fruit—into the cocktail as they mix it.

GLASSWARE: Rocks glass

GARNISH: None

KANJI IN THE EVENING

If you have one, use a smoke gun to add a fragrant cherry-wood aroma to a mix—the smoke also looks mighty classy.

1 oz. Appleton Estate signature blend rum

¾ oz. Ron Zacapa 23 rum

1¾ teaspoons Yellow Chartreuse

½ oz. Aperol

½ oz. Pink Pepper & Pomegranate Syrup (see recipe)

¾ oz. fresh lime juice

1. Place all of the ingredients in a cocktail shaker, fill it two-thirds of the way with ice, and shake vigorously until chilled.

2. Place an ice sphere in a rocks glass and double strain the cocktail over it.

3. If desired, use a smoke gun filled with cherrywood chips to smoke the drink; don't leave it running too long: 10 to 15 seconds is about right.

PINK PEPPER & POMEGRANATE SYRUP: Place 2 cups 100 percent pomegranate juice in a saucepan and bring it to a boil. Add 2 tablespoons sugar, 1 tablespoon fresh lemon juice, and 1 teaspoon whole pink peppercorns, reduce the heat, and simmer the mixture for 30 minutes. Remove the pan from heat and let the syrup cool completely. Strain before using or storing.

GLASSWARE: Brandy snifter

GARNISH: Cinnamon, strip of orange peel

ZU ZU

The #9 mix is poised to become your favorite secret weapon, adding richness, spice, and an eye-catching froth to drinks.

2 oz. Diplomatico Reserva rum

½ oz. Plantation pineapple rum

½ oz. fresh lime juice

½ oz. fresh grapefruit juice

½ oz. fresh orange juice

1 oz. #9 (see recipe)

4 pineapple chunks

1. Place the ingredients in a blender, add ½ cup ice, and puree until smooth.

2. Pour the cocktail into the brandy snifter, garnish with the cinnamon and orange peel, and enjoy.

#9: Place 2 oz. Reàl ginger syrup and 1 oz. almond paste in a container and stir until combined. Stir in 1 teaspoon St. Elizabeth allspice dram and use immediately or store in the refrigerator.

GLASSWARE: Rocks glass
GARNISH: None

DOT LINE

A rich, fruity, spicy cocktail that's good any time of day.

¼ oz. ground Kenyan coffee

1⅓ oz. Bacardi Carta Blanca rum

⅔ oz. umeshu

1 bar spoon Pedro Ximénez sherry

1 bar spoon St-Germain

Dash of balsamic vinegar

---

1. Place a coffee dripper over a mixing glass, line the coffee dripper with a filter, and place the coffee in the filter.

2. Pour the rum, umeshu, sherry, and St-Germain over the coffee and let them drip into the glass.

3. Add the balsamic vinegar to the mixing glass, then ice, and stir to incorporate.

4. Strain the cocktail over an ice sphere into the rocks glass and enjoy.

GLASSWARE: Rocks glass, stored in the freezer

GARNISH: Olive

HAVANA MARTINI

Takao Mori a legend in the Tokyo cocktail world, is the master of the Martini (see pages 218–219 for a look at his recipe and technique). At one point, a customer challenged him to make him a Martini using rum, and after around 20 iterations, he landed on a winner.

3 oz. Havana Club 7 Year rum, chilled in the freezer

½ teaspoon Valdespino inocente fino sherry

Drop of orange bitters

1 strip of lemon peel

1. Place the rum, sherry, and bitters in a mixing glass containing large ice cubes and stir briskly for 30 seconds.
2. Pour the cocktail into the chilled rocks glass, making sure

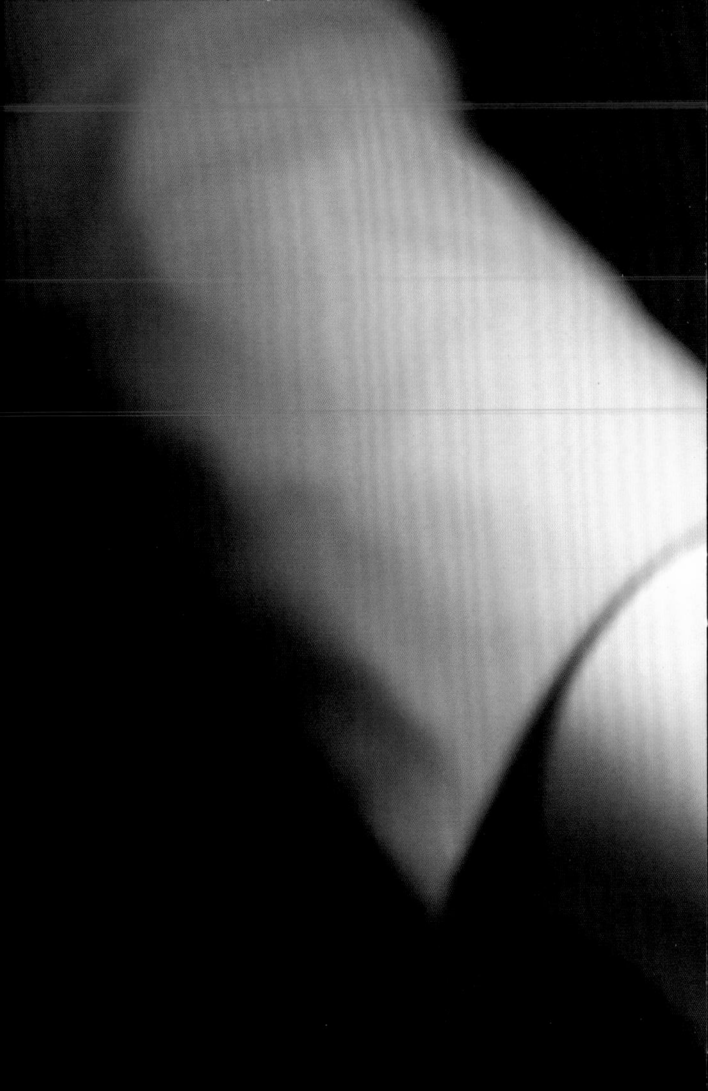

Takao Mori is known throughout Japan as the master of the Martini, a reputation that has sustained despite a number of twists and turns.

Early in his career, back in the 1960s and '70s, he was making Martinis with a high-proof Gordon's gin, as were most of his peers. Gradually, though, he began to feel that the quality of the gin was slipping, and he asked Japan's three big beverage companies to find him something better. In 1987, Kirin Seagram suggested Boodles and it was a bull's-eye. It had weight, depth, and the touch of sweetness that he says a Martini gin needs. It was also tough enough to survive in a freezer.

Mori likes to chill the gin to -4°F, at which point, he says, "It's dead."

He then revives it with a dash of orange bitters, a splash of vermouth, and 100 brisk rotations with ice in a mixing glass. He stirs not to chill the drink, but to wake it up, bringing the temperature up to around 19°F, with each rotation sending a little more water into the mix.

Japan's top bar associations all asked Mori to make Martinis for their conferences, and word quickly got around. By the time he opened his eponymous bar in 1997, he was using more Boodles than anyone else in the world, and the makers showed their gratitude by furnishing him with their formula.

Then a US firm bought Boodles and tweaked the recipe. They made it gentler, more approachable, and Mori immediately stopped using it. He would have stopped making Martinis altogether, but his customers demanded them. He was stuck with gins he felt were too simple, too light.

Salvation of a sort came with the arrival of Japanese gins. The makers of Ki No Bi offered to create a spirit to Mori's taste. He traveled to Kyoto to help develop it, armed with his Boodles recipe, and in 2017, his 50th year as a bartender, the Ki No Bi Mori edition made its debut. Precisely what's in it, nobody will say, but Mori finally had his dream gin again.

Well, not quite.

Ki No Bi's base spirit is made from rice, not grain like Boodles, and Mori says that means it's too light to live in a freezer, and thus too light for his signature stir. So he chills it in the fridge and gives it just 50 rotations. But he says Suntory's roku gin is rugged enough. It goes in the freezer and comes back to life with the full hundred stirs. So there are now two Mori Martinis. The Ki No Bi Martini is deliciously complex and fun. The Suntory version is deep and precise. Since this latter gin is the only one available to the public, that's the version provided here.

GLASSWARE: Cocktail glass

GARNISH: Olive

Drop of orange bitters

3½ oz. Suntory roku gin (chilled to −4°F)

½ teaspoon Mancino secco vermouth

1 strip of lemon peel

---

1. Place three large ice cubes in a mixing glass, cover them with water, and stir. Strain the water from the mixing glass.

2. Add the drop of bitters.

3. Pour the gin into the mixing glass, add the vermouth, and stir rapidly 100 times.

4. Strain into a cocktail glass, skewer the olive on a cocktail pick, and garnish the cocktail with it.

5. Express the strip of lemon peel over the drink, discard the lemon peel, and enjoy.

ROASTED RUM MANHATTAN

Two long-aged spirits, two vermouths, and some roasted green tea make for a long and layered after-dinner cocktail

---

1½ oz. Hōjicha Rum (see recipe)

1 bar spoon Daniel Bouju XO Cognac

½ oz. Carpano antico formula sweet vermouth

1 bar spoon Carpano punt e mes vermouth

---

1. Place all of the ingredients in a mixing glass and stir.

2. Add ice to the mixing glass and stir once.

3. Strain the cocktail into the cocktail glass, garnish with the griottine or black cherry, and enjoy.

HŌJICHA RUM: Place 1 tablespoon loose-leaf hōjicha tea in 1 (750 ml) bottle of Ron Zacapa 23 rum and let it steep over-night. Strain before using or storing.

GLASSWARE: Highball glass

GARNISH: None

CHARTREUSE MOJITO

The Mojito's strongest attributte—its breezy, refreshing nature—is also its weakness, threatening to make any encounter with it forgettable. The numerous directions that Chartreuse gives to the tastebuds eliminate that downside, while preserving all of the advantages.

---

1 bar spoon caster (superfine) sugar

Handful of fresh spearmint

1 lime wedge

1 oz. Bacardí rum

⅔ oz. Green Chartreuse

Club soda, to top

---

1. Place the sugar and spearmint in the highball glass and muddle.

2. Squeeze the juice from the lime wedge into the glass, remove the lime pulp, discard it, and place the spent lime wedge in the glass.

3. Add the rum, Chartreuse, and cracked ice to the glass and top with club soda.

4. Stir until chilled and enjoy.

I WISH I WAS IN NEW ORLEANS

For those who get it, each year is filled with moments where one looks longingly toward the Crescent City.

⅔ oz. Havana Club 7 Year rum

⅓ oz. Giffard wild elderflower liqueur

1¼ teaspoons fresh lime juice

2 dashes of Peychaud's bitters

Brut Champagne, to top

---

1. Place all of the ingredients, except for the Champagne, in a cocktail shaker, fill it two-thirds of the way with ice, and shake vigorously until chilled.

2. Strain the cocktail into the Champagne flute and top with Champagne.

3. Garnish with the strip of lemon peel and enjoy.

GLASSWARE: Nick & Nora glass

GARNISH: 2 star anise pods, cinnamon stick

HUMMINGBIRD-CUSIN

An autumnal tea transformed by the slight funk of cachaça.

---

2 to 3 cinnamon sticks

Blossoms from 2 stems of amaranth

3 star anise pods

2 oz. warm water

Honey Syrup (see page 80), to taste

1½ oz. cachaça

1 bar spoon fresh lemon juice

---

1. Place the cinnamon sticks, amaranth, star anise pods, and warm water in a glass and let the mixture steep for 5 minutes.

2. Strain the tea into a mixing glass, add the cachaça and lemon juice, and stir to combine.

3. Taste the cocktail, add Honey Syrup to taste, and stir to incorporate. Add ice to the mixing glass and stir until chilled.

4. Strain the cocktail over ice into the Nick & Nora glass, garnish with the star anise pods and cinnamon stick, and enjoy.

GLASSWARE: Clay bowl

GARNISH: Dusting of matcha powder

LOST IN TRANSLATION

Perhaps it is only a trick of the mind, but the green hue lent by the matcha powder seems to make the grassy nature of cachaça and the green apple notes in shochu all the more powerful.

---

1 oz. cachaça

1 oz. shochu

½ oz. fresh lime juice

¾ oz. Simple Syrup (see page 26)

¼ teaspoon matcha powder

¾ oz. egg white

---

1. Place all of the ingredients in a cocktail shaker and dry shake for 10 seconds.

2. Fill the cocktail shaker two-thirds of the way with ice and shake vigorously until chilled.

3. Double strain the cocktail into the clay bowl, top with the dusting of matcha powder, and enjoy.

THE DRY SHAKE

Egg white provides cocktails with a beautiful and delectable foam, but it can be difficult to incorporate due to its viscous nature. To combat this issue and ensure that the egg white is emulsified, many bartenders will shake the ingredients without any ice before adding ice and shaking the cocktail to chill it. Some bartenders will even place the spring from a Hawthorne strainer in the shaker while dry shaking, believing that it acts as a whisk. In recent years, the reverse dry shake—straining a shaken cocktail, discarding the ice, returning the cocktail to the shaker, and shaking it again—has gained favor, as it is believed to produce a more robust foam. But there are some who feel the reverse dry shake has gained momentum due primarily to the rise of social media, as it creates a foam that looks better, but lacking in texture. Try both methods and see which you prefer.

SWEATER WEATHER

A fusion of two classics, the Hot Toddy and the Dark and Stormy.

1½ oz. aged rum

¾ oz. rye whiskey

½ oz. Cointreau

½ oz. Ginger Syrup (see page 30)

¾ oz. fresh lemon juice

---

1. Place all of the ingredients in a cocktail shaker, fill it two-thirds of the way with ice, and shake vigorously until chilled.

2. Strain over ice into the double rocks glass, garnish with the lemon twist and clove, and enjoy.

New Orleans in the early 1900s, after absinthe was banned in the United States, and though the green fairy is no longer prohibited, Herbsaint remains the choice for tiki lovers and rum enthusiasts.

---

1 oz. Plantation 3 stars rum

½ oz. gin

¾ oz. fresh lemon juice

1 oz. pineapple juice

1 oz. guava puree

¾ oz. Ginger Syrup (see page 30)

1 bar spoon Herbsaint

4 dashes of Angostura bitters

---

1. Place all of the ingredients, except for the bitters, in a mixing glass, add 2 oz. crushed ice, and stir until foamy.

2. Pour the contents of the mixing glass into the Collins glass, add the bitters, and top with more crushed ice.

3. Garnish with the pineapple leaves and orchid and enjoy.

GLASSWARE: Collins glass
GARNISH: None

SALTY DOUG

This rum-based riff on the Salty Dog has an incredible mouthfeel, thanks to use of the Breville Juice Fountain, which spins fast enough to provide additional texture.

Grapefruit Salt (see recipe), for the rim

1½ oz. Diplomatico mantuano rum

½ oz. fresh lime juice

¼ oz. Agave Syrup (see recipe)

3 to 4 fresh grapefruits, skin and pith removed, flesh cut into chunks

---

1. Wet the rim of the Collins glass and coat it with the Grapefruit Salt.

2. Place the rum, lime juice, and Agave Syrup in the juicer cup of a Breville Juice Fountain.

3. Turn the juicer on high, add the grapefruit chunks, and blitz to combine.

4. Add ice to the rimmed glass, pour the cocktail into it, and enjoy.

GRAPEFRUIT SALT: Take 1 cup of grapefruit pulp left over from the juicer and spread it on a baking sheet. Place the baking sheet in a food dehydrator, set it to 160°F, and dehydrate until the pulp is completely dry (you can also do this in an oven set to warm). Grind the dehydrated pulp with a spice grinder until it is fine. Combine with 4 cups kosher salt and store in an airtight container.

AGAVE SYRUP: Place ¾ cup agave nectar and ¼ cup water in a saucepan and bring to a simmer. Cook until the syrup has the desired consistency, remove the pan from heat, and let the syrup cool completely before using or storing.

CHILI CHILLY BANG BANG

Don't be fooled by the cheeky pun—this cocktail features some impressive imagination and craft.

---

2 oz. Angostura 5-Year rum

1 oz. Angostura bitters

1 oz. Ginger Syrup (see page 30)

1 oz. Coco López cream of coconut

1½ oz. fresh lime juice

¾ oz. pineapple juice

Handful of fresh mint

2-second squirt of sriracha

---

1. Place all of the ingredients in a blender, add 10 oz. crushed ice, and puree on high until smooth.

2. Pour the cocktail into the tiki mug and enjoy.

GLASSWARE: Rocks glass

GARNISH: None

WHEN THE MAN COMES AROUND

A rummy spin on the classic Martinez cocktail.

---

small strip of lime peel

2 oz. Guyana rum

oz. Cocchi Vermouth di Torino

¼ oz. Luxardo maraschino liqueur

0 drops of Angostura bitters

3 dashes of orange bitters

4 drops of absinthe

2 lemon twists

---

1. Express the lime peel over a mixing glass and drop it into the glass.

2. Add the remaining ingredients, except for the lemon twists, to the mixing glass, fill it two-thirds of the way with ice, and stir until chilled.

3. Strain over a large ice cube into the rocks glass, express the lemon twists over the cocktail, discard them, and enjoy.

SECRET LIFE OF PLANTS

Floral and fruity with a thick mouthfeel, the oolong also adds a light, verdant note that elevates this entire cocktail.

1½ oz. lightly aged rum

¾ oz. Mango & Oolong Syrup (see recipe)

¾ oz. fresh lime juice

¼ oz. Orgeat (see page 57)

¼ oz. falernum

10 drops of 20 Percent Saline Solution (see recipe)

Dash of absinthe

---

1. Place all of the ingredients in a cocktail shaker, fill it two-thirds of the way with ice, and shake vigorously until chilled.

2. Fill the tumbler with crushed ice and strain the cocktail over it.

3. Top with more crushed ice, garnish with the fresh Thai basil, and enjoy.

MANGO & OOLONG SYRUP: Place ¾ cup water in a saucepan and heat it to 195°F. Add ¼ cup loose-leaf oolong tea and steep for 5 minutes. Strain the tea, discard the leaves, and return the tea to the saucepan. Add 30 oz. mango puree, 30 oz. white sugar, 1 (12 oz.) can of mango nectar, and a scant 2½ teaspoons citric acid (12 grams) and warm the mixture over low heat, stirring to dissolve the sugar. When the syrup is well combined, remove the pan from heat and let it cool completely before using or storing.

20 PERCENT SALINE SOLUTION: Place 1 oz. salt in a mason jar and add warm water until the mixture measures 5 oz. Stir to combine and let the solution cool before using or storing.

THE POWER OF ONE

Simple, luscious, and surprisingly complex, thanks to the Appleton Estate rum.

---

2 oz. Appleton Estate reserve blend rum

1 oz. coconut milk

1 oz. fresh lime juice

1 oz. Demerara Syrup (see page 36)

---

1. Place all of the ingredients in a cocktail shaker, fill it two-thirds of the way with ice, and shake vigorously until chilled.

2. Fill the Collins glass with crushed ice and strain the cocktail over it.

3. Top with more crushed ice, garnish with the shaved fresh ginger, and enjoy.

GLASSWARE: Zombie mug or tiki mug

GARNISH: ½ passion fruit husk, 3 pineapple leaves, passion fruit, coconut sugar, rum, absinthe, dusting of cinnamon

PIN-UP ZOMBIE

The garnishes may seem involved, but they forge the necessary connections between the numerous flavors here.

---

1 oz. Bacardí añejo cuatro rum

1 oz. Pusser's gunpowder proof rum

2 teaspoons Santa Teresa 1796 rum

½ oz. Quaglia Liquore cherry liqueur

2 teaspoons Quaglia Liquore pine liqueur

2 teaspoons falernum

1 oz. Passion Fruit Syrup (see page 59)

¾ oz. fresh pink grapefruit juice

½ oz. fresh lime juice

---

1. Place all of the ingredients in a cocktail shaker, fill it two-thirds of the way with ice, and shake vigorously until chilled.

2. Fill the mug with crushed ice and strain the cocktail over it.

3. Add more crushed ice and place the passion fruit husk and pineapple leaves on top.

4. Add a spoonful of passion fruit and a generous pinch of coconut sugar to the cocktail.

5. Combine 2 teaspoons each of rum and absinthe, pour the mixture into the passion fruit husk, and light it with a long match. Sprinkle cinnamon over the flames and, cautiously, enjoy the cocktail.

VERY HUNGRY MANZANILLA

Paraphrased from the famed children's book by Eric Carle, *The Very Hungry Caterpillar*, this very grown-up drink has plenty of depth, belying the green hue.

1¼ oz. Plantation 3 stars rum

½ oz. Amontillado sherry

¾ oz. fresh lime juice

½ oz. Sage & Mint Agave (see recipe)

Seltzer, to top

---

1. Place all of the ingredients, except for the seltzer, in a cocktail shaker, fill it two-thirds of the way with ice, and shake vigorously until chilled.

2. Double strain over ice into the Collins glass and top the cocktail with seltzer.

3. Garnish with the perforated sprig of mint and the candy caterpillar and enjoy.

SAGE & MINT AGAVE: Place 9 oz. agave nectar, 2 ½ oz. water, 50 fresh mint leaves, and 8 fresh sage leaves in a blender and puree until smooth. Strain the mixture through cheesecloth before using or storing.

GLASSWARE: Rocks glass

GARNISH: Lime wedge, sprig of mint

EL CUCO

A refreshing, ice cold take on the Navy Grog, a tiki classic. A tip for this and any other drink jammed with crushed ice: use a chopstick to bore a hole through the ice so you can access the drink with a straw.

---

1 oz. Appleton Estate signature blend rum

½ oz. Hamilton Guyana 86 rum

½ oz. Caña Brava 7 Year rum

½ oz. El Dorado 3 Year rum

¾ oz. fresh lime juice

¾ oz. grapefruit juice

¾ oz. Honey & Ginger Syrup (see page 113)

Seltzer, to top

---

1. Place all of the ingredients, except for the seltzer, in a cocktail shaker, fill it two-thirds of the way with ice, and shake vigorously until chilled.

2. Fill the rocks glass with crushed ice and strain the cocktail over it.

3. Top the cocktail with the seltzer, garnish it with the lime wedge and fresh mint, and enjoy.

RUM / 237

FINISHING TOUCHES

You can call it a day after mixing a cocktail and straining it into a glass, but a drink isn't truly complete until the garnish has been added. Able to provide a burst of color as well as an aroma and flavor that ties the entire package together, knowing how to finish strong is the final piece of the mixology puzzle.

While the cocktail world, particularly those drinks that reside in the realm of tiki, is home to increasingly fabulous garnishes, there's no need for you to fashion dolphins out of bananas or soak a slice of lime in overproof rum so that it can be set alight in the glass. Simply knowing how to cut a citrus peel so that you get all of the bright zest and none of the bitter pith, or how to affix a lime wedge on the glass's rim so a guest can easily squeeze its juice into their drink is enough to seal the deal. When done correctly, the garnish gilds the lily—adding an aesthetic component that transforms the process of crafting cocktails into theater, and an accent that helps the other elements shine.

In order to transform citrus into satisfactory garnishes, always wash and dry the fruit thoroughly before starting to work with it. And to ensure that they do not become dried out, try to make citrus-based garnishes as close to cocktail hour as possible.

Beyond that, a few tools and some practice are required. Common kitchen workhorses like the paring knife, vegetable peeler, box grater, and microplane will serve you well. But if you want to take things a step further, the following specialized tools can clear the way.

Channel knife: The U-shaped blade of this classic bar tool is essential if you're looking to create long and swanky strips of zest.

Pronged tip bar knife: The long, thin handle makes elaborate cuts a cinch, while the tip makes it easy to spear cherries and olives.

"Y" garnish peeler: This professional piece of kit bears close resemblance to a safety razor, and the "Y" stands for "yes" in terms of pulling off whatever duty it is charged with.

To create a typical strip of citrus zest, place a just-sharpened paring knife between the zest and white pith and twist the fruit, while applying moderate pressure, until you have removed the required amount of zest.

For cocktails that require a wider strip of zest employ the same method but use a vegetable peeler. The resulting strip can then be held above the cocktail and twisted into a tight spiral to express the aromatic oils into the drink. Once you've done that, either discard the twist or drop it into a drink to add a burst of color and a touch of refinement.

While the twist requires the most finesse and technique of the citrus garnishes, the others do need a bit of care if you want to get them right. To cut a proper wedge of citrus, slice a ¼ inch off each end of a citrus fruit. Next, cut the fruit in half, lengthwise, and set one of the halves, cut side down, on your cutting board. Finally, slice it at an angle, lengthwise, and you should have a perfect little wedge. Cut a slit in the midsection of the wedge so that it can rest on the rim of a glass.

For a citrus wheel, cut the fruit in half crosswise and then make a parallel cut about ⅛ to ¼ inch above the initial cut. Cut the wheel from the edge to the center so that it can rest on the glass's rim.

Using herbs such as sprigs of mint, rosemary, or thyme as a garnish requires nothing more than your hands. Since you are utilizing an herb for its aroma as much as anything, lay the sprigs or leaves in the palm of one hand and give them a good smack with the other before placing them in the cocktail. This bit of sternness will whip an herb into shape, activating its essential oils.

When garnishing a cocktail with olives, it is traditional to place three on a skewer. One is consumed following the first sip, and the remaining two after the last. If that seems like too many, simply drop one into the cocktail. Olives can also be stuffed with various ingredients to add another layer of flavor. While the sweet pimento remains the mostcommon by far, garlic cloves, almonds, blue cheese, jalapeño peppers, and even anchovies have become frequent fillings for olives.

And, finally, if a cocktail calls for a maraschino cherry, steer clear of the ruby red version that the supermarket has accustomed you to. That chemically saturated, super-sweet variety can't hold a candle to the true maraschino king. Luxardo. Made from the sour marasca cherries that only grow in the sandy soils of Croatia's Dalmatian mountain range, they are preserved in a syrup consisting only of sugar and the marasca's juice. A Luxardo cherry has a deep-red, almost-purple color that lends a touch of class to a cocktail, as well as a rich flavor that carries notes of almond. They are far more expensive than the syrupy charlatan, but worth every penny if you are serious about making the best cocktails you can.

GLASSWARE: Rocks glass

GARNISH: Dehydrated banana chip

TUESDAY CLUB

A soft, sweet drink with exhilarating spicy notes and a deep vein of vanilla. If you can't procure this exact brand of CBD syrup, add a drop or two of regular CBD oil to a Banana Syrup (see page 250).

---

3 dashes of Bittermens 'Elemakule Tiki bitters

1¼ oz. El Dorado 3 year rum

¾ oz. Spiced Rum (see recipe)

¼ oz. Behind This Wall Banana CBD Syrup

Pear calvados, to mist

---

1. Place the bitters, rums, and a large block of ice in the rocks glass.

2. Add the syrup and stir until the cocktail is chilled.

3. Pour a bit of pear calvados into a spray bottle and mist the cocktail with it.

4. Garnish with the dehydrated banana chip and enjoy.

SPICED RUM: Place 6 whole cloves, 1 cinnamon stick, 6 allspice berries, and 10 whole black peppercorns in a saucepan and toast over medium-low heat until the spices are fragrant, about 1 minute, shaking the pan occasionally. Remove the pan from heat, add ¼ cup Demerara Syrup (see page 36) and 1 tablespoon Wray & Nephew rum, and stir to combine. Split a vanilla bean in half, scrape the seeds into the rum mixture, and add the pod as well. Add a bottle of Wray & Nephew rum so that the mixture is easy to pour, pour it into a large mason jar, and then add another bottle of Wray & Nephew rum. Store the jar in a cool, dark place and let the mixture steep until the flavor is to your liking, shaking the jar occasionally. Strain the rum before using or storing at room temperature.

GOOD FORTUNE

The acidity of the oranges, yuzu, and lime blends elegantly with the smoky sweetness of the Zacapa rum, and the touch of heat from the Vanilla & Chile Syrup really rounds off the drink.

1⅜ oz. Ron Zacapa 23 rum

¾ oz. umeshu

2 teaspoons orange marmalade

1 oz. fresh lime juice

½ oz. Vanilla & Chile Syrup (see recipe)

---

1. Chill the cocktail glass in the freezer.

2. Place all of the ingredients in a cocktail shaker, fill it two-thirds of the way with ice, and shake vigorously until chilled.

3. Double strain the cocktail into the chilled cocktail glass.

4. Hold the strip of orange peel about 2 inches above a lit match for a couple of seconds. Twist and squeeze the peel over the lit match, while holding it above the cocktail and taking care to avoid the flames. If desired, rub the torched peel around the rim of the glass, garnish the cocktail with it, and enjoy.

VANILLA & CHILE SYRUP: Place 1 cup water in a saucepan and bring it to a boil. Add 2 cups demerara sugar and stir until it has dissolved. Remove the pan from heat and stir in 2 chopped jalapeño chile peppers. Halve 4 vanilla beans, scrape the seeds into the syrup, and add the pods as well. Stir to combine and let the syrup cool completely. Strain before using or storing.

THE TOUGH GET GOING

Topping this twist on the Mai Tai with the balanced but indulgent flavor of Santa Teresa rum is more than enough to reinvigorate that classic.

1½ oz. Royal Standard dry rum

½ oz. fresh orange juice

½ oz. Orgeat (see page 57)

½ oz. curaçao

¼ oz. fresh lime juice

½ oz. Santa Teresa 1796 rum

---

1. Place all of the ingredients, except for the Santa Teresa rum, in a cocktail shaker, fill it two-thirds of the way with ice, and shake vigorously until chilled.

2. Fill the large tumbler with crushed ice and strain the cocktail over it.

3. Float the Santa Teresa rum on top of the cocktail, pouring it over the back of a spoon.

4. Garnish with the wide strip of orange peel and enjoy.

GLASSWARE: Collins glass

GARNISH: Pineapple leaves, dehydrated lime wheel

ISLAND HOPPER

Freshly pressed Hawaiian sugarcane produces some fantastic rum, and fortunately, there is a small crop of exciting distilleries that are taking advantage of the local produce, like Oahu's KōHana Distillers.

---

1 oz. Don Q Cristal rum

½ oz. KōHana Kea agricole

½ oz. Hibiscus Syrup (see page 144)

½ oz. fresh lemon juice

¾ oz. pineapple juice

2 oz. ginger beer

---

1. Place all of the ingredients, except the ginger beer, in a cocktail shaker, fill it two-thirds of the way with ice, and shake vigorously

2. Place the ginger beer in the Collins glass, strain the cocktail into the glass, and fill it with crushed ice.

3. Garnish the cocktail with the pineapple leaves and dehydrated lime wheel and enjoy.

GLASSWARE: Tumblers

GARNISH: None

EGG NOG PUNCH

Save this one for the holiday party, as it comfortably makes several dozen servings.

---

4 cups buttermilk

8 cups whole milk

6 cups heavy cream

3 cups aged rum

2¼ cups VSOP Brandy

1 tablespoon pumpkin spice

6 eggs, yolks and whites separated

1½ cups sugar

Salt, to taste

---

1. In a large container, combine the buttermilk, milk, heavy cream, rum, brandy, and pumpkin spice.

2. Combine the egg yolks and 1 cup of sugar in the work bowl of a stand mixer fitted with the whisk attachment. Whisk the mixture until it is a vibrant yellow. Add the egg yolk mixture to the mixture in the large container and whisk to incorporate.

3. Clean the stand mixer's work bowl and then place the egg whites and remaining sugar in it. Whip until soft peaks form.

4. Gradually fold the egg white mixture into the liquid mixture, which will create a more luscious texture.

5. Chill the egg nog in the refrigerator for 1 hour before serving.

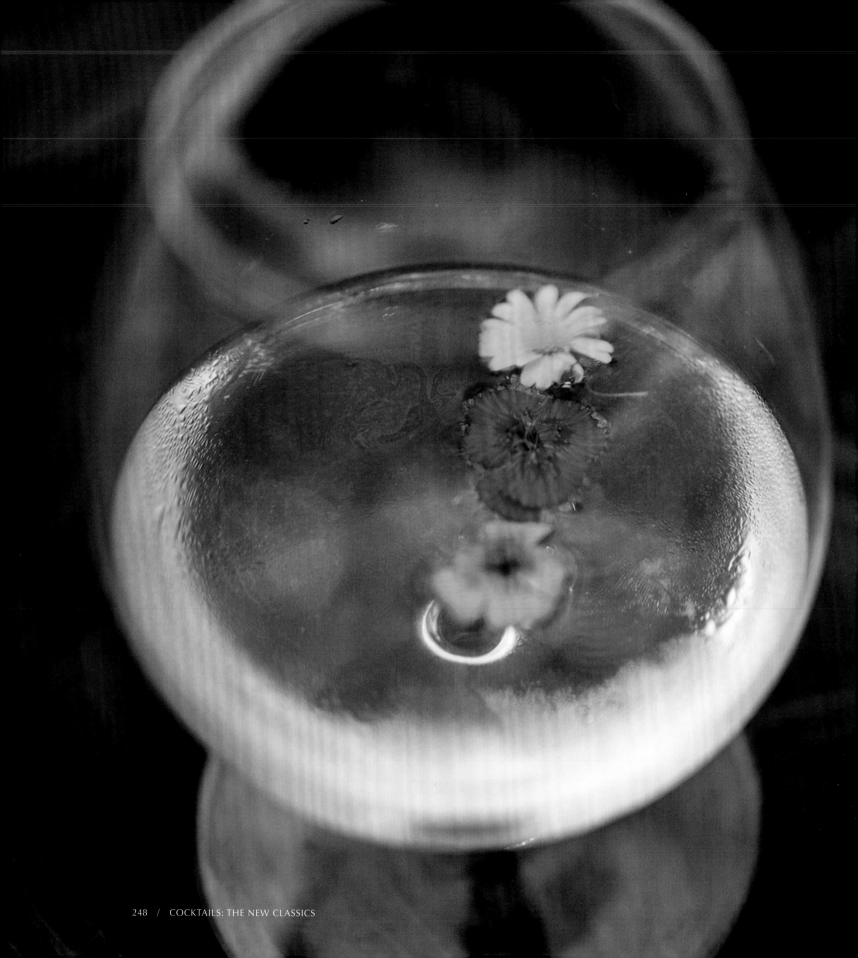

GLASSWARE: Brandy snifter
GARNISH: Edible flowers

BE MY WINE

Light-bodied rum provides a great base for this exotic cocktail, which is defined by floral notes, spice and citrus from the falernum, and the inimitable White Wine Reduction.

1½ oz. Don Q rum

¾ oz. White Wine Reduction (see recipe)

¾ oz. falernum

1 spritz of lavender oil

---

1. Place all of the ingredients in a mixing glass, fill it two-thirds of the way with ice, and stir until chilled.

2. Double strain the cocktail into the brandy snifter, garnish with edible flowers, and enjoy.

WHITE WINE REDUCTION: Place 1 cup dry white wine and ½ cup sugar in a saucepan and bring to a simmer. Cook until the mixture has reduced by half, remove the pan from heat, and let the reduction cool completely before using or storing.

This cocktail's wintry look belies the verdant taste, allowing it to make a lasting impression.

1½ oz. cachaça

½ oz. sake

1 oz. Banana Syrup (see recipe)

½ oz. yuzu juice

¼ oz. fresh lemon juice

2 crushed shiso leaves

1 egg white

Club soda, to top

1. Place all of the ingredients, except for the club soda, in a cocktail shaker and dry shake for 10 seconds.

2. Add ice, shake vigorously until chilled, and double strain over ice into the rocks glass.

3. Top with club soda, garnish with the ground tea leaves, and enjoy.

BANANA SYRUP: Place 5 peeled bananas and 4 cups Simple Syrup (see page 26) and bring to a boil. Cook for 5 minutes, reduce heat to medium–low, and simmer for 15 minutes. Strain the syrup and let cool completely before using or storing.

GLASSWARE: Collins glass

GARNISH: Fresh mint, Lemongrass Syrup

SOUTH POINTE SWIZZLE

Let people try and guess what forms the backbone of this drink, and take pleasure in how taken aback they are when they find out it's rum-based.

---

2 oz. Bacardí superior rum

1 oz. fresh lime juice

¾ oz. Lemongrass Syrup (see recipe)

5 fresh mint leaves

Dash of Angostura bitters

---

1. Place all of the ingredients, except for the bitters, in a Collins glass, add crushed ice, and use the swizzle method to mix the drink: place a swizzle stick between your hands, lower the swizzle stick into the drink, and quickly rub your palms together to rotate the stick as you move it up and down in the drink. When frost begins to form on the outside of the glass, the drink is ready.

2. Add crushed ice to fill and top with the bitters.

3. Garnish with the fresh mint and syrup and enjoy.

LEMONGRASS SYRUP: Place 1 cup water and 1 cup sugar in a saucepan and bring to a boil, stirring to dissolve the sugar. Remove the pan from heat, add 2 coarsely chopped lemongrass stalks, and let the mixture steep for 24 hours. Strain before using or storing.

GLASSWARE: Tiki mug

GARNISH: Fresh mint, star anise pod

SAILOR'S GUILLOTINE

A wonderfully orchestrated, albeit unexpected, cocktail.

¼ oz. absinthe

1 oz. rhum agricole

½ oz. falernum

½ oz. Green Chartreuse

1 oz. fresh pineapple juice

¾ oz. fresh lime juice

---

1. Place all of the ingredients in a cocktail shaker, fill it two-thirds of the way with crushed ice, and shake vigorously until chilled.

2. Pour the contents of the shaker into the tiki mug and top the cocktail with more crushed ice.

3. Garnish the cocktail with the fresh mint and star anise pod and enjoy.

THE EXPEDITION

A celebration of the ingredients that Donn Beach, the tiki pioneer, was exposed to during the travels of his youth, and celebrated for the rest of his ife—coffee and bourbon from New Orleans, fresh citrus from California, and rum and spices from the Caribbean.

---

2 oz. Hamilton Guyana 86 rum

1 oz. bourbon

¼ oz. Bittermens New Orleans coffee liqueur

1 oz. fresh lime juice

½ oz. Cinnamon Syrup (see page 127)

½ oz. Honey Syrup (see page 80)

¼ oz. Vanilla Syrup (see recipe)

2 oz. seltzer

---

1. Place all of the ingredients in a cocktail shaker, add crushed ice, and flash mix with a hand blender.

2. Pour the contents of the shaker into the tiki mug.

3. Garnish with the edible orchid and enjoy.

VANILLA SYRUP: Place 1 cup water in a small saucepan and bring it to a boil. Add 2 cups sugar and stir until it has dissolved. Remove the pan from heat. Halve 1 vanilla bean and scrape the seeds into the syrup. Cut the vanilla bean pod into thirds and add the pieces to the syrup. Stir to combine, cover the pan, and let the mixture sit at room temperature for 12 hours. Strain the syrup through cheesecloth before using or storing.

THE TIKI REVIVAL

Of all the trends that have come about through the the modern cocktail movement, the resurgence of tiki drinks is among the most surprising.

Tiki is a strange amalgamation of craft, imagination, escapism, and cultural appropriation. Looking at it from certain vantage points, it seems to be little more than an exceptionally effective marketing strategy. From others, tiki veers dangerously close to tacky. From another point of view, it is a craft that rewards precision and daring, one that without a doubt produces some of the best cocktails in the world today. In truth, tiki is a heady mix of all of these things, and, while we are primarily concerned with the mixological aspects in this book, a true appreciation can only come through taking a close look at the elements that fostered the enigmatic essence of these cocktails.

The tiki conversation can only start in one place, with one man: Don the Beachcomber. Born Ernest Gantt in 1907, Gantt ripped through an inheritance galivanting around the world and drinking in everything from the South Pacific to the Caribbean. Eventually, Gantt's funds ran out, and he found himself in Los Angeles, making ends meet with a series of odd jobs—including one that involved him lending the artifacts he'd gathered during his travels to movie studios looking to give their sets a bit of authenticity. By 1933, Gantt had saved enough to open his own place, and turned a small room that had been a tailor shop into Don's Beachcomber, a charmingly run-down rum shack in the middle of Hollywood. Adorned with his numerous treasures and featuring cocktails that pushed the flavors Gantt had fallen in love with during his prodigal years, the bar was an instant hit.

Gantt, who eventually leaned fully into his construction and changed his name to Donn Beach (the bar's name was also changed, to Don the Beachcomber), was certainly a marketing wizard. But he was also a daring mixologist who not only had impeccable taste, but an artist's willingness to tinker and revise until the final product was just right. He discovered that by blending rums, he could give a cocktail added complexity and a strong backbone. By incorporating spices,

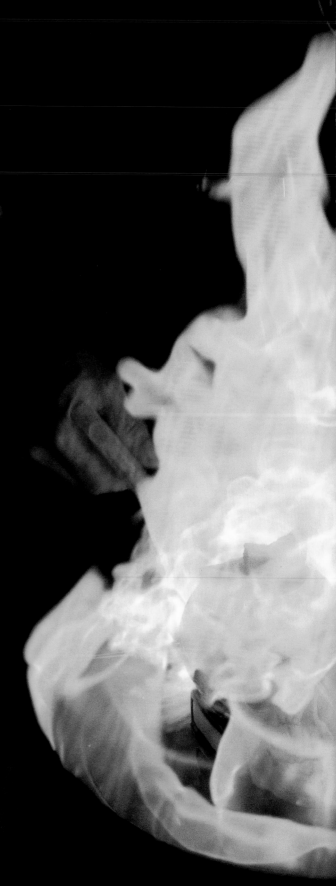

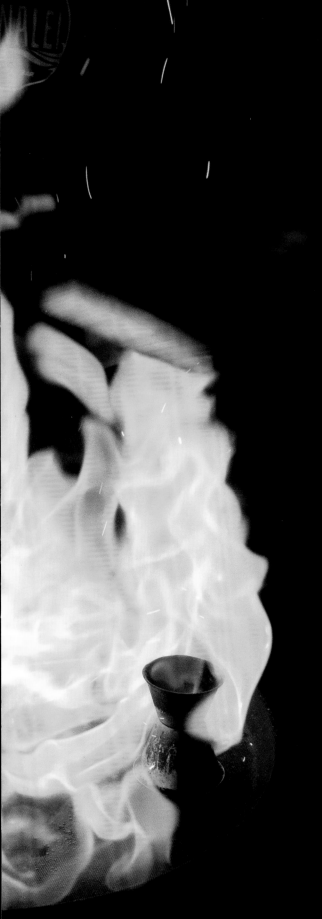

fresh juices, and sweeteners, he could transport his guests a world away from the hustle and bustle of the city outside the door. While the tiki palate continues to grow, it was Beach's love for citrus, pineapple, passion fruit, maple syrup, grenadine, allspice liqueur, peach brandy, coffee, Angostura, and, of course, rum that provided its foundation.

The exotic building blocks of Donn's cocktails went into unmarked bottles, coded in a manner that only he knew— not even the Beachcomber's bartenders knew exactly what was in the drinks people revered them for crafting. Unfortunately for Beach, and fortunately for the rest of us, his security measures proved not to be enough. In the 1930s, Don the Beachcomber had a customer who was so eager and so inquisitive about what was happening that the employees branded him "The Rope Hanger." That watchful regular was Vic Bergeron, an Oakland restaurateur, and while Vic's vigilance quickly got him bounced, he took Donn's blueprint and used it to make over his own restaurant. The rest is history. Vic used everything he'd soaked up to expand Beach's vision, adding spirits such as gin, pisco, and tequila to the mix, and also incorporating the beguiling French syrup orgeat (it's pronounced "ore-zha"), an innovation that led to the creation of the Mai Tai, what many believe to be the ultimate tiki cocktail. But Bergeron did more than just expand what could be considered tiki—he expanded its reach. Ever open the menu at a Chinese-American restaurant and be charmed and confused by the page of cocktails bearing an exotic look and occasionally ridiculous names? That is another piece of Vic's legacy, as he was the first to understand that this hybrid cuisine was the perfect partner for tropical-leaning cocktails, and put his theory into practice at a new restaurant in San Francisco—Trader Vic's. This restaurant was quickly the toast of the Bay Area, and his establishments soon spread around the country, an expansion aided in large part by the Polynesian craze that had seized the United States.

For a while tiki's momentum seemed unstoppable, but eventually, the craft that Beach and Bergeron built their empires upon was lost, and the cocktails carrying the tiki torch stopped seeking balance and began to emphasize the strong and sugary elements, and eschewed fresh fruit and juices for prefabricated blends that were closer to what a car mechanic would employ than a mixologist. This decline, combined with an increasingly thoughtful culture that was uncomfortable with what tiki had co-opted from island peoples and cultures, pushed tiki to the dusty corners of cocktail culture.

And there tiki stayed, a kitschy symbol of a bygone era, its appeal apparent to just a handful of true believers. Eventually, one of those believers, Jeff "Beachbum" Berry, would devote himself to cracking Beach's codes, talking with old bartenders who had come of age in tiki's heyday. In 1997, Berry compiled the early results of this work in *Beachbum Berry's Grog Log*. The book did well enough to bring Berry's project to the attention of Jennifer Santiago, the daughter of a former Beachcomber bartender. Jennifer handed Berry her father's notebook, and though it was in Donn's arcane codes (featuring bespoke and inscrutable ingredients such as Donn's Mix and Spices #4), Berry persisted, poring over this tome for years. The books that have resulted from this study, including *Intoxica* and *Beachbum Berry's Sippin' Safari*, returned tiki to respectability in cocktail culture, and inspired Martin Cate (see page 31) and others to honor and expand on Donn Beach's vision.

RABO DE GALO

The sweetness of rum is a perfect match for the rich, nutty flavor of the Cashew Syrup.

1½ oz. Don Papa rum

½ oz. sweet vermouth

¾ oz. dry vermouth

½ oz. Cashew Syrup (see recipe)

2 dashes of Angostura bitters

---

1. Place all of the ingredients in a cocktail shaker, fill it two-thirds of the way with ice, and shake vigorously until chilled.

2. Strain over a large ice cube into the rocks glass, garnish with the orange twist, and enjoy.

CASHEW SYRUP: Preheat the oven to 350°F. Place 1 cup cashews on a baking sheet, place them in the oven, and toast for 5 minutes. Remove the cashews from the oven and set them aside. Place 1 cup sugar and 1 cup water in a saucepan and bring to a boil, stirring to dissolve the sugar. Place the syrup and cashews in a blender and puree until smooth. Strain the syrup and let it cool completely before using or storing.

SLOE SUNSET

When shopping for pomegranate liqueur, Pama is the one and only choice. Although you could just substitute grenadine (see page 61) and funk this up with another rum.

___

oz. Hibiscus-Infused Rum (see recipe)

oz. sloe gin

oz. pomegranate liqueur

oz. fresh grapefruit juice

oz. fresh lemon juice

oz. Demerara Syrup (see page 36)

___

Place all of the ingredients in a cocktail shaker, fill it two-thirds of the way with ice, and shake vigorously until chilled.

Fill the Collins glass with crushed ice and strain the cocktail over it.

Garnish the cocktail with the edible flowers and enjoy.

HIBISCUS-INFUSED RUM: Place ⅔ oz. dried hibiscus blossoms and 4 cups Smith & Cross rum in a large mason jar and steep for 48 hours. Strain before using or storing.

COTTON MOUTH KILLER

For the rum blend, consider using a few lighter rums such as The Real McCoy 3 Year and Havana Club with some heavier, aged pot still rums like Plantation xaymaca to create a drink with an incredibly smooth profile.

1¾ oz. rum blend

2 teaspoons Rothman & Winter orchard apricot liqueur

2 teaspoons Galliano

2 teaspoons Demerara Syrup (see page 36)

1 oz. apple juice

1⅜ oz. guava juice

2 bar spoons Blue Wray & Nephew (see recipe)

---

1. Place all of the ingredients, except for the Blue Wray & Nephew, in a cocktail shaker, fill it two-thirds of the way with ice, and shake vigorously until chilled.

2. Fill the tiki mug with crushed ice and strain the cocktail over it.

3. Top the cocktail with additional crushed ice and gently sti

4. Drizzle the Blue Wray & Nephew over the cocktail and enjoy

BLUE WRAY & NEPHEW: Place ¾ cup Wray & Nephew rum and ¼ cup blue curaçao in a mason jar and stir to combine. Use immediately or store at room temperature.

GLASSWARE: Rocks glass

GARNISH: Passion fruit slice, fresh mint

RUM BA BA

Named after the French cake, this cocktail is not as sweet as you'd think considering the ingredients. Think of this as part of an adult version of milk and cookies.

1½ oz. Appleton Estate Reserve Blend rum

1½ oz. heavy cream

1 oz. Orgeat (see page 57)

½ oz. fresh lemon juice

1¼ oz. passion fruit puree

2 dashes of Peychaud's Bitters

---

1. Place all of the ingredients in a cocktail shaker, fill it two-thirds of the way with ice, and shake vigorously until chilled.

2. Fill a rocks glass with ice and double strain the cocktail over it.

3. Garnish with the passion fruit slice and fresh mint and enjoy.

2. Fill the tumbler with crushed ice and double strain the cocktail over it.

3. Garnish the cocktail with the lit joint—unless, of course, it's illegal or you don't abide—and enjoy.

PINEAPPLE-INFUSED RUM: Place 10 ½ oz. chopped pineapple and a 750 ml bottle of rum in a mason jar and steep for 1 week. Strain before using or storing at room temperature.

GLASSWARE: Rocks glass

GARNISH: None

MOJITO DE PIÑA

Swapping basil in for the mint and incorporating the swee
and-sour taste of pineapple maintains the Mojito's famed
freshness, but provides a renewed, vibrant dimension tha
should be present in any riff.

1½ oz. Pineapple-Infused Rum (see page 264)

1 oz. fresh lime juice

1 oz. pineapple puree

5 fresh basil leaves, torn in half

1½ tablespoons caster (superfine) sugar

1 oz. ice water

1. Place all of the ingredients in a cocktail shaker, fill it
   two-thirds of the way with ice, and shake vigorously
   until chilled.

2. Pour the contents of the shaker into the rocks glass and
   enjoy.

DEPARTMENT OF AGRICOLE

The Burnt Sugar Simple Syrup adds the necessary note of bitterness to the otherwise sweet proceedings.

1½ oz. unaged rhum agricole

1 oz. fresh lime juice

½ oz. falernum

¼ oz. cold-brew coffee

¼ oz. coffee liqueur

¼ oz. Burnt Sugar Simple Syrup (see recipe)

---

1. Place all of the ingredients in a cocktail shaker, fill it two-thirds of the way with ice, and shake vigorously until chilled.

2. Double strain the cocktail into the coupe.

3. Garnish with the lemon twist and enjoy.

BURNT SUGAR SIMPLE SYRUP: Place 1 cup sugar and ½ cup water in a saucepan and bring to a boil over medium-high heat, stirring constantly, until the mixture becomes caramel-colored. Remove the pan from heat, add ½ cup warm water —carefully, because the syrup will steam and bubble—and stir to incorporate. Let the syrup cool completely before using or storing.

GLASSWARE: Cocktail glass

GARNISH: None

EYES OF MY MIND

If you want a frothier version, combine the ingredients with crushed ice and give a few pulses with an immersion blender.

1½ oz. aged rum

¾ oz. fresh lime juice

½ oz. crème de cacao

½ oz. Demerara Syrup (see page 36)

---

1. Chill the cocktail glass in the freezer.

2. Place all of the ingredients in a cocktail shaker, fill it two-thirds of the way with ice, and shake vigorously until chilled.

3. Strain into the chilled cocktail glass and enjoy.

CABLE CAR

A classic sour gets a contemporary update with the addition of baking spices.

---

1 oz. Edgefield three rocks spiced rum

½ oz. triple sec

½ oz. Simple Syrup (see page 26)

½ oz. fresh lemon juice

---

1. Chill the cocktail glass in the freezer.

2. Place all of the ingredients in a cocktail shaker, fill it two-thirds of the way with ice, and shake vigorously until chilled.

3. Strain into the chilled cocktail glass, garnish with the cinnamon and nutmeg, and enjoy.

VODKA

Vodka is the tofu of spirits. And, despite whatever you may think about tofu, this comparison is meant to be a compliment, in that vodka's lack of a distinctive flavor allows it to find a comfortable place beside a stunning amount of other ingredients, a perfect spirit for cocktails. You can pair it with damn near anything, as evidenced by its presence in a diverse group of cocktails that spans from Martinis to Bloody Marys and White Russians. Vodka's versatility also means that you can literally add it to any type of fruit juice and voila . . . you have a cocktail—vodka and orange juice, vodka and cranberry juice (a Cape Cod), or vodka and grapefruit juice. It plays well with many other spirits and complements whatever it is added to, which is not something you can say about other types of alcohol.

Vodka can be made from anything that can be fermented to create alcohol. This includes grains such as rye, barley, and wheat, as well as vegetables like beets and potatoes. The location of the distillery and what the distillers have the easiest access to will generally govern what is used to create vodka. Many countries use grain to make their vodka, with potatoes being a close second. Each imparts different advantages.

Potato's high level of starch imparts a creamy, oily mouthfeel and a light, natural sweetness to vodka, while grains are thought to produce a cleaner spirit that is easier to work with.

That ease puts many in the craft cocktail space off, to the point that they despise vodka, and refuse to work with it. But, as you know, in the contemporary cocktail world, a hardline stance is simply the progenitor of considerable opportunities. As you'll see, a number of mixologists have seized upon them, filling that open space with unusual ingredients and innovative blends that will delight vodka enthusiasts, and win over those who are skeptical of the spirit.

SAPPORO

A cocktail that the renowned Japanese bartender Tatsuro Yamazaki created when Sapporo, his hometown, was gearing up to host the 1972 Winter Olympics. As you'll discover, it's one of the few drinks from that decade whose taste is timeless.

---

1 oz. vodka

2 bar spoons Amaretto

2 bar spoons Green Chartreuse

2 bar spoons dry vermouth

---

1. Place all of the ingredients in a mixing glass, fill it two-thirds of the way with ice, and stir until chilled.

2. Strain into the cocktail glass, garnish with the green cocktail cherry, and enjoy.

GLASSWARE: Cocktail glass

GARNISH: Strip of grilled yuzu peel

MATCHA MARTINI

Grilled zest and a splash of juice is all it takes to tell your senses that this is a yuzu drink.

1½ oz. vodka

1 oz. fresh grapefruit juice

1 bar spoon fresh yuzu juice

1 bar spoon matcha powder

---

1. Place all of the ingredients in a cocktail shaker, fill it two-thirds of the way with ice, and shake vigorously until chilled.

2. Strain into the cocktail glass, garnish with the strip of grilled yuzu peel, and enjoy.

1½ oz. Shiso Cordial (see recipe)

1⅓ oz. fresh lemon juice

⅔ oz. Butterfly Pea Water (see recipe)

---

1. Place all of the ingredients in a cocktail shaker, fill it two-thirds of the way with ice, and shake vigorously until chilled.

2. Strain into the coupe, garnish with the sesame oil, and enjoy.

SHISO CORDIAL: Place 1 cup water, 1 cup sugar, and 1 oz. vodka in a saucepan and warm over medium heat, stirring to dissolve the sugar. Remove the pan from heat, add 20 shiso leaves, and steep for 1 hour. Stir in 1 gram of citric acid and strain before using or storing.

BUTTERFLY PEA WATER: Steep 1 cup loose-leaf butterfly pea tea in 4 cups hot water for 10 minutes. Strain before using or storing.

COPPER CUP #4

Earthy, spicy, and herbal, this cocktail is a resounding answer to those who doubt vodka's capacity to produce next-level cocktails.

2 oz. Absolut elyx vodka

¾ oz. St-Germain

¼ oz. freshly pressed ginger juice

¾ oz. fresh lemon juice

¼ oz. Hibiscus Syrup (see page 144)

1. Place all of the ingredients in a cocktail shaker, fill it two-thirds of the way with ice, and shake vigorously until chilled.

2. Fill the copper cup with crushed ice, strain the cocktail over it, and top with more crushed ice.

3. Garnish with the slice of ginger and orchid blossom and enjoy.

THE PINEAPPLE

It's not just a clever nickname—this cocktail is chock-full of the pineapple's unmatched mix of sweet and tart.

2½ oz. Absolut elyx vodka

2 oz. Pineapple Mix (see recipe)

1 oz. pineapple puree

¾ oz. fresh lemon juice

Peychaud's bitters, to top

---

1. Place all of the ingredients, except for the bitters, in a cocktail shaker, fill it two-thirds of the way with ice, and shake until chilled.

2. Fill a copper cup with crushed ice and strain the cocktail over it.

3. Top more crushed ice and drizzle bitters over the cocktail.

4. Garnish with the torched sprig of fresh rosemary and enjoy.

PINEAPPLE MIX: Place 1¼ cups oloroso sherry, ½ cup Salted Vanilla Syrup (see recipe), 1 cup Rosemary Syrup (see recipe), ½ cup pineapple puree, ½ cup Simple Syrup (see page 26), and ½ bottle Bittermens 'Elemakule Tiki Bitters in a mason jar and stir to combine. Use immediately or store in the refrigerator.

SALTED VANILLA SYRUP: Place 3 pinches of salt, 2 cups Simple Syrup, and 1 tablespoon pure vanilla extract in a saucepan and bring to a simmer, stirring to dissolve the salt. Remove the pan from heat and let the syrup cool completely before using or storing.

ROSEMARY SYRUP: Place 1 cup water in a saucepan and bring to a boil. Add 1 cup sugar and 4 sprigs of fresh rosemary and stir until the sugar has dissolved. Remove the pan from heat and let the syrup cool completely. Strain before using or storing.

PRIDE

The Pride is inspired by Oscar Wilde's two favorite drinks, absinthe and Champagne, with the former's aroma being articulated by the combination of Jasmine-Infused Vodka and the star anise extract.

---

1 oz. Jasmine-Infused Vodka (see recipe)

1 oz. Lime & Sage Cordial (see recipe)

Vignoble Guillaume Flûte Enchantée sparkling wine, to top

Star anise extract, to mist

---

1. Place the vodka and cordial in a cocktail shaker, fill it two-thirds of the way with ice, and shake vigorously until chilled.

2. Strain into the coupe and top with sparkling wine.

3. Place the star anise extract in an atomizer and mist the cocktail with it.

4. Tie the paper strip to the stem of the glass, and enjoy.

JASMINE-INFUSED VODKA: Place a 750 ml bottle of vodka and 3 tablespoons of jasmine pearl tea in a mason jar and steep for 3 to 4 hours. Strain before using or storing.

LIME & SAGE CORDIAL: Place 11 oz. fresh lime juice and 21 oz. caster (superfine) sugar in a saucepan and bring to a simmer, stirring to dissolve the sugar. Stir in 1½ oz. chopped lime peel and 1½ oz. fresh sage leaves, cook for 5 minutes, and remove the pan from heat. When the mixture has cooled, pour it into a mason jar, cover, and let the mixture steep for 4 hours. Strain the cordial before using or storing in the refrigerator.

DORSET DONKEY

A very British take on the Moscow Mule.

1¾ oz. Black Cow vodka

1¾ teaspoons syrup from jar of Morello cherries

½ oz. fresh lime juice

Fever-Tree ginger ale, to top

---

1. Place the vodka, syrup, and lime juice in the highball glass and fill it with ice. Stir for a few seconds.

2. Top with the ginger ale and gently stir.

3. Garnish with the sage leaves and either a berry or a Morello cherry and enjoy.

STRANGER THINGS

The fruitiness supplied by the strawberry-laced vodka and passion fruit puree makes the nice, dry finish provided by the Prosecco essential to the drink.

1⅜ oz. Strawberry Tea–Infused Vodka (see recipe)

1⅜ oz. passion fruit puree

¾ oz. Simple Syrup (see page 26)

Prosecco, to top

---

1. Place the vodka, passion fruit puree, and syrup in a cocktail shaker, fill it two-thirds of the way with ice, and shake vigorously until chilled.

2. Double strain into a lightbulb glass or champagne flute and top with Prosecco.

3. Garnish with the raspberry and enjoy.

STRAWBERRY TEA–INFUSED VODKA: Place 3 bags of strawberry tea and a 750 ml bottle of vodka in a mason jar, shake vigorously, and steep for 24 hours. Remove the tea bags before using or storing.

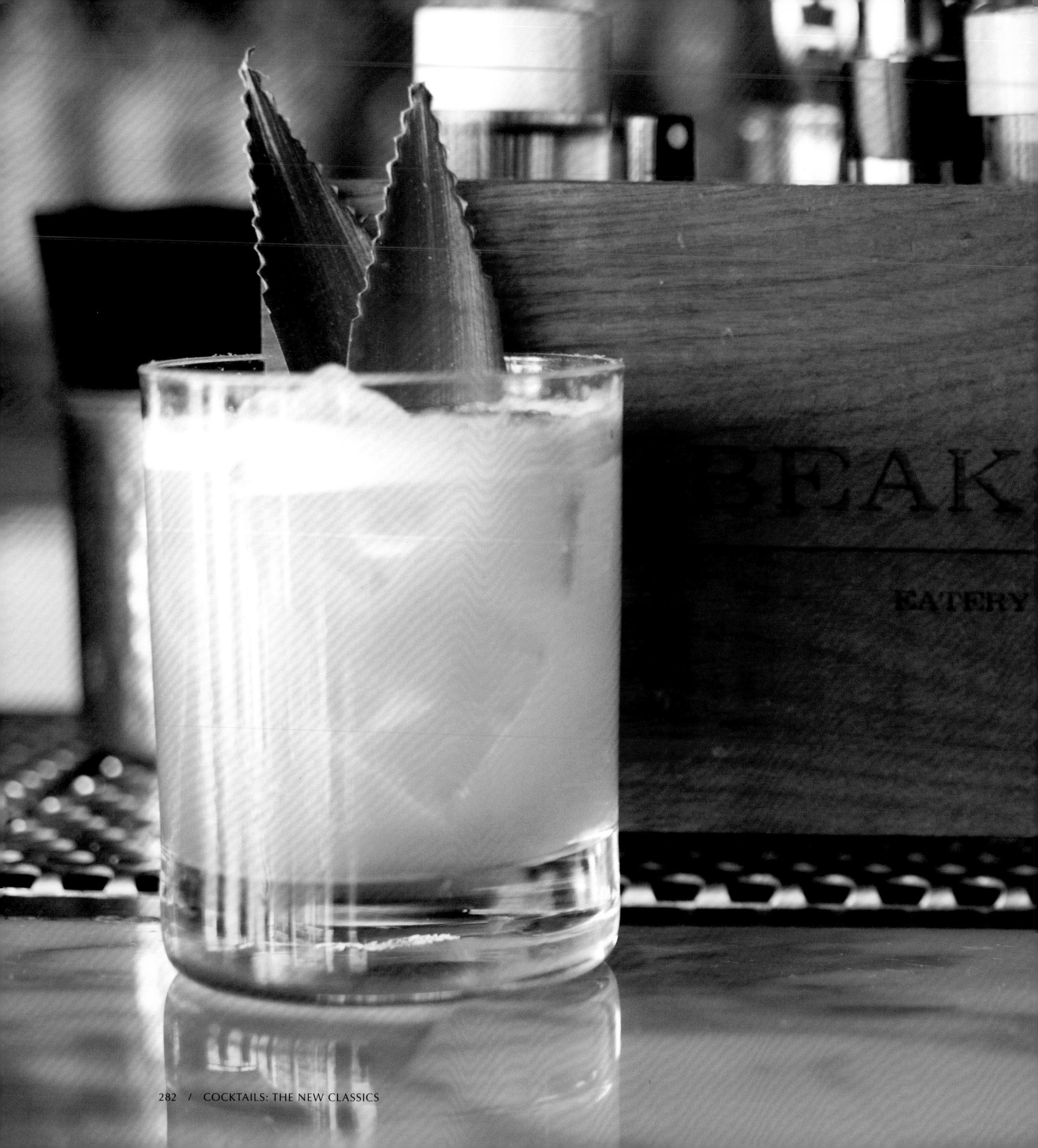
BEAK
EATERY

THE HALLIWELL

When the temperature starts to rise, a cocktail built around strawberries and mint is the key to keeping cool.

1½ oz. Stoli vodka

½ oz. Cocchi Americano Rosa

1 oz. Ginger Syrup (see page 30)

1 oz. fresh lemon juice

1 oz. strawberry puree

8 fresh mint leaves

---

1. Place all of the ingredients in a cocktail shaker, fill it two-thirds of the way with ice, and shake vigorously until chilled.

2. Double strain over ice into the Collins glass, garnish with fresh mint, and enjoy.

GLASSWARE: Copper cup
GARNISH: Pineapple leaf, dehydrated lime wheel

WYNWOOD MULE

If grilling pineapple is next level, smoking it is the highest.

1½ oz. vodka

1 oz. fresh lime juice

¾ oz. Smoked Pineapple Syrup (see recipe)

2 oz. ginger beer

---

1. Place all of the ingredients in the copper cup, fill it with crushed ice, and gently stir.

2. Garnish with the pineapple leaf and dehydrated lime wheel and enjoy.

SMOKED PINEAPPLE SYRUP: Place 4 to 6 whole pineapples in a smoker, set it to 220°F, and smoke the pineapples until they are charred, 3 to 4 hours. Remove from the smoker and let them cool. Chop the pineapples, making sure to reserve any juices, and weigh them. Place the pineapples and any juices in a saucepan and add 60 percent of their weight in water. Bring to a rolling boil and cook for 15 minutes. Stir in 40 percent of the pineapples' weight in sugar and simmer for 45 minutes. Place the mixture in a food processor and blitz until pureed. Strain the syrup and let it cool completely before using or storing. If you're looking for a quicker way to get a smoky flavor into pineapple, slice the pineapples and cook them on a charcoal grill for 15 minutes. Remove them from the grill and follow the same method recommended above.

SACRED LOTUS

Tamarind adds a tangy note of citrus to the vodka and is balanced by the St-Germain. Top that off with Prosecco and fruit, and you get an easy yet elevated sangria.

---

1 oz. Tamarind–Infused Vodka (see recipe)

1 oz. St-Germain

Prosecco, to top

---

1. Place the vodka and St-Germain in the wine glass, add ice, and top with the Prosecco.

2. Garnish with the cucumber slice, berries, lemon wheel, and orange slice and enjoy.

TAMARIND-INFUSED VODKA: Place ⅓ cup peeled and deseeded tamarind pulp and 4 cups vodka in a large mason jar and store in a cool, dark place for 1 week, shaking it daily. Strain before using or storing.

ESPRESSO MARTINI

Here, the famously too sweet-too rich-too everything dessert Martini is transformed into something thoughtful and well-composed.

---

1 oz. Grey Goose la vanille vodka

1 oz. cold-brew coffee concentrate

¾ oz. Pedro Ximénez sherry

---

1. Place all of the ingredients in a cocktail shaker, fill it two-thirds of the way with ice, and shake vigorously until chilled.

2. Quickly double strain the cocktail into the cocktail glass, to retain as much of the frothy crema as possible. If the straining doesn't occur quickly enough, the crema will stick to the ice in the shaker, which will result in a drink that looks rather disappointing.

3. Garnish with a thin line of the salt-and-coffee blend and enjoy.

ISLE OF VIEW

Take the example provided by this drink to heart—a bit of Maldon can go a long way in terms of adding depth to a cocktail.

---

2 oz. Absolut Elyx vodka

¾ oz. Orgeat (see page 57)

¾ oz. fresh lime juice

¾ oz. Passion Fruit Syrup (see page 59)

Pinch of Maldon sea salt

---

1. Place all of the ingredients in a cocktail shaker, fill it two-thirds of the way with ice, and shake vigorously until chilled.

2. Fill the rocks glass with crushed ice and strain the cocktail over it.

3. Garnish the cocktail with the nutmeg and fresh mint and enjoy.

APOTHECARY

Why would you use lime when you have sudachi, a tart green Japanese citrus fruit? And if you ever find shell ginger leaf, a key part of cuisine in Okinawa, Japan, it adds a wonderful green note.

---

20 juniper berries

¼ shell ginger leaf

2 oz. vodka

⅔ oz. fresh sudachi juice

2 bar spoons Simple Syrup (see page 26)

---

1. Use a mortar and pestle to grind the juniper berries and shell ginger leaf into a fine powder.

2. Place the mixture in a cocktail shaker. Add the remaining ingredients and ice and shake vigorously until chilled.

3. Double strain into the cocktail glass, garnish with the sudachi wheel and shell ginger leaf, and enjoy.

CHOCOLATE MARTINI

It's essential to use a room-temperature vodka here, because a chilled one will cause the chocolate to set and throw the drink's texture and flavor off. Also, a light touch when expressing the strip of yuzu peel over the drink is recommended.

---

2 tablespoons grated Valrhona Chocolate (56 percent)

1 oz. Grey Goose vodka, at room temperature

1 oz. heavy cream

1 bar spoon Truffle-Infused Honey (see recipe)

1 strip of yuzu peel

---

1. Fill a saucepan halfway with water and bring it to a simmer. Place the chocolate in a heatproof bowl, place it over the simmering water, and stir until it has melted.

2. Place all of the ingredients, except for the strip of yuzu peel, in a cocktail shaker, fill it two-thirds of the way with ice, and shake vigorously until chilled.

3. Double strain into the cocktail glass, express the strip of yuzu peel over the cocktail, discard the yuzu peel, and enjoy.

TRUFFLE-INFUSED HONEY: Fill a saucepan halfway with water and bring it to a simmer. Place the honey in a heatproof bowl and place it over the simmering water until it is warm. Shave some winter truffle into the honey, stir to combine, and remove the bowl from heat. Cover the bowl and let the mixture steep for at least 24 hours. Strain before using or storing.

THE PROPER WAY TO
EXPRESS A CITRUS PEEL

Hold the citrus peel between your thumb
and index or middle finger, at the same
height as the rim of the glass and 2 or 3
inches away, and with the zest pointing
away. Squeeze the edges together and
waft the peel near the cocktail—you don't
want to do it directly above it, because
the citrus notes will spray forward while
bitter oils fall straight down.

When you plunge a red-hot poker into the glass, the temperature of the drink jumps immediately, some of the liquid evaporates and you end up with a toasted flavor that proves irresistible.

---

1 oz. vodka

2 oz. tomato juice

⅔ oz. apple juice

2 drops of balsamic vinegar

½ teaspoon unsalted butter

1 bar spoon honey

---

1. Place all of the ingredients in a heatproof glass and stir to combine.

2. Heat a poker to almost 1,000°F and then plunge it into the drink for 30 seconds.

3. Pour the cocktail into the Hot Toddy glass and enjoy.

ARCADIA

If a drink could turn into a cake if you baked it, this would be it.

⅓ oz. Finlandia vodka

2 bar spoons of Midori melon liqueur

2 bar spoons of Kahlúa

⅓ oz. heavy cream

1 egg yolk

1. Place all of the ingredients in a cocktail shaker, fill it two-thirds of the way with ice, and shake vigorously until chilled.

2. Strain the cocktail into the coupe, garnish with the crushed chocolate and fresh mint, and enjoy.

GLASSWARE: Rocks glass
GARNISH: Fried curry leaf

WHISTLE PODU

Rasam, a spicy-and-sour tomato soup traditional in southern India, keys this brilliant twist on the Bloody Mary.

---

2 oz. Smoked Rasam (see recipe)

2 oz. vodka

¾ oz. honey

¾ oz. fresh lime juice

1 oz. club soda

---

1. Place all of the ingredients in a mixing glass, stir to combine, and then carbonate the cocktail.

2. Pour the cocktail over ice into the rocks glass, garnish with the fried curry leaf, and enjoy.

SMOKED RASAM: Dice 15 tomatoes, place them in a saucepan, and cook over medium heat for about 20 minutes. Add coriander seeds, curry leaves, mustard seeds, and Masala Water (see recipe), stir to combine, and remove the pan from heat. Place the saucepan in a large roasting pan. Place hickory wood chips in a ramekin, coat a strip of paper towel with canola oil, and insert it in the center of the wood chips. Set the ramekin in the roasting pan, carefully light the wick, and wait until the wood chips ignite. Cover the roasting pan with aluminum foil and smoke the rasam for 1 hour.

MASALA WATER: Place 2 oz. dried mango in a bowl of hot water and soak it for 30 minutes. Place the re-hydrated mango, 3 oz. cilantro, 3 green chile peppers, ½ teaspoon black pepper, ¼ teaspoon grated fresh ginger, and 2 teaspoons dried mint in a food processor and blitz until the mixture is a smooth paste. Stir the paste into 4 cups water and use as desired.

Infused with pear, rose, chamomile, lemon verbena, lavender, rosemary, coriander, and citrus peel, Square One botanical vodka stands far above the rest of its shelfmates when it comes to flavor.

---

8 fresh basil leaves

1 (heaping) teaspoon sugar

1¼ oz. Square One botanical vodka

½ oz. Green Chartreuse

¼ oz. Maurin Quina

¾ oz. fresh lime juice

---

1. Chill the coupe in the freezer.

2. Place the basil leaves and sugar in a cocktail shaker and gently muddle.

3. Add the remaining ingredients and ice and shake vigorously until chilled.

4. Double strain into the chilled coupe, garnish with the Luxardo maraschino cherries, and enjoy.

GLASSWARE: Coupe

GARNISH: Fresh mint

AMELIA

A drink for those who can't have a cocktail that's too tart.

1½ oz. vodka

1 oz. Blackberry Puree (see recipe)

¾ oz. St-Germain

½ oz. fresh lemon juice

---

1. Chill the coupe in the freezer.

2. Place all of the ingredients in a cocktail shaker, fill it two-thirds of the way with ice, and shake vigorously until chilled.

3. Strain the cocktail into the chilled coupe, garnish with fresh mint, and enjoy.

BLACKBERRY PUREE: Place ¼ lb. fresh or thawed frozen blackberries, 2 tablespoons caster (superfine) sugar, 2 tablespoons water, and 2 tablespoons fresh lemon juice in a blender and puree until smooth. Strain before using or storing.

GLASSWARE: Collins glass
GARNISH: English Cucumber slices, Pickled Purple Cucumbers (see recipe), Pickled Huckleberries (see recipe)

CUCUMBER COLLINS

Along with the Chartreuse Swizzle, this is one of the Bay Area's signature 21st century drinks.

1½ oz. Square One cucumber vodka

½ oz. fresh lemon juice

¼ oz. fresh yuzu juice

½ oz. Simple Syrup (see page 26)

1½ oz. soda water, chilled

---

1. Place the vodka, juices, and syrup in the short half of a Boston shaker. Fill it to the top with ice and seal it.

2. Shake just a few times to mix the cocktail. Unseal the shaker, leaving everything in the larger half.

3. Add the chilled soda water to the mixture and swirl it around a few times to incorporate.

4. Pour the contents of the shaker into the Collins glass, garnish with the cucumbers and huckleberries, and enjoy.

PICKLED PURPLE CUCUMBERS: Place 3 cups Pickled Huckleberry brine and 3 cups thinly sliced English cucumbers in a large container, cover it, and refrigerate for 24 hours before using.

PICKLED HUCKLEBERRIES: Place 6 cups unseasoned rice vinegar, 2 cups mirin, and 2 cups cooking sake in a large saucepan and bring to a boil. Add 3 cups sugar and stir to dissolve. Add 2 lbs. wild huckleberries and bring to a boil. Remove the pan from heat and let the mixture cool. Strain, making sure to reserve 3 cups of brine for the Pickled Purple Cucumbers, before using or storing.

GLASSWARE: Pint glass

GARNISH: Dried apple ring

BEET CONNECTION

A quartet of fresh juices and a chile-enriched vodka make this a good cocktail to turn to in the fall, when you've tired of the ubiquitous pumpkin-flavored drinks.

---

2 oz. Chile-Infused Vodka (see recipe)

1½ oz. freshly pressed beet juice

1½ oz. freshly pressed apple juice

½ oz. fresh lemon juice

¼ oz. freshy pressed ginger juice

¼ oz. Simple Syrup (see page 26)

¼ oz. orange juice

Pinch of kosher salt

---

1. Place all of the ingredients in a cocktail shaker, fill it two-thirds of the way with ice, and shake vigorously until chilled.

2. Strain over ice into the pint glass, garnish with the dried apple ring, and enjoy.

CHILE-INFUSED VODKA: Place 4 cups vodka, 3 deseeded and sliced jalapeño chile peppers, and 5 deseeded dried chipotle chile peppers in a large mason jar and let the mixture steep for 24 hours, shaking occasionally. Strain before using or storing.

GLASSWARE: Coupe

GARNISH: English cucumber wheel

TRANQUILLO

Pear, with its subtle vanilla notes, carries this light and refreshing cocktail.

---

1 lime wedge

Dash of caster (superfine) sugar

2 English cucumber wheels

2 oz. Lovejoy vodka

½ oz. pear nectar

---

1. Place the lime wedge, sugar, and 6 ice cubes in a cocktail shaker and muddle.

2. Add the remaining ingredients and more ice and shake vigorously until chilled.

3. Strain the cocktail into the coupe, garnish with the cucumber wheel, and enjoy.

GLASSWARE: Copper mug

GARNISH: Fresh curly parsley, dehydrated pear slice, confectioners' sugar

MOMBAI MULE

A beautiful twist on the Moscow Mule that emphasizes two elements—cardamom and cinnamon—that both agree with the ginger beer, and can stand up to its strong flavor.

1¾ oz. Cardamom-Infused Vodka (see recipe)

1¾ oz. apple juice

⅞ oz. pear puree

½ oz. fresh lime juice

1¾ teaspoons Cinnamon Syrup (see page 127)

Fentimans ginger beer, to top

---

1. Place ice in the copper mug and build the drink in the mug, adding the ingredients in the order they are listed.

2. Stir until chilled, garnish with the fresh parsley, dehydrated pear slice, and confectioners' sugar, and enjoy.

CARDAMOM-INFUSED VODKA: Place 10 green cardamom pods and a 750 ml bottle of vodka in a large mason jar and store in a cool, dark place for 2 weeks, shaking every few days. Strain before using or storing.

CHERVONA WINE

Who says vodka isn't much in the flavor department? This Hunter's Vodka will convince you and other naysayers that this stance largely results from a lack of imagination.

1½ oz. Hunter's Vodka (see recipe)

1½ oz. dry red wine

½ oz. sweet vermouth

½ oz. Simple Syrup (see page 26)

---

1. Place all of the ingredients in a cocktail shaker, fill it two-thirds of the way with ice, and shake vigorously until chilled.

2. Strain over ice into the rocks glass and express the orange twist over the cocktail.

3. Garnish with the orange twist and a dusting of nutmeg and enjoy.

HUNTER'S VODKA: Place 1½ teaspoons allspice berries, 1½ teaspoons juniper berries, ½ teaspoon black peppercorns, ½ teaspoon coriander seeds, ½ teaspoon fenugreek seeds, 1 cinnamon stick, 1 piece of a star anise pod, and 1 clove in a skillet and toast over medium heat until aromatic, shaking the pan frequently. Place the toasted spices in a large mason jar and add a 750 ml bottle of vodka. Cover and let the mixture steep for 4 days in a dark, cool place. Strain, stir in 1 tablespoon maple syrup, and shake the bottle to combine. Chill in the freezer for 1 hour before using.

EAST OF EDEN

A creamy, floral, delicately sweet, and bright cocktail that tastes like an elegant, lavender-infused Piña Colada.

1½ oz. vodka

½ oz. coconut rum

¼ oz. heavy cream

½ oz. egg white

½ oz. fresh lemon juice

½ oz. Simple Syrup (see page 26)

2 dashes of lavender bitters

---

1. Place all of the ingredients in a cocktail shaker, fill it two-thirds of the way with ice, and shake vigorously until chilled.

2. Strain into the coupe and enjoy.

GLASSWARE: Rocks glass

GARNISH: Lemon wedge

MY RESCUE

The rare beer cocktail that can hang with the big boys.

1½ oz. Monopolowa vodka

1½ oz. Allagash White or other wit-style beer

½ oz. fresh lemon juice

1 bar spoon Honey & Toasted Spice Syrup (see recipe)

¾ oz. Aperol

---

1. Place all of the ingredients in a cocktail shaker, fill it two-thirds of the way with ice, and shake vigorously until chilled.

2. Strain over ice into the rocks glass, garnish with the lemon wedge, and enjoy.

HONEY & TOASTED SPICE SYRUP: Place 30 coriander seeds and 5 cloves in a skillet and toast them over medium heat until aromatic, shaking the pan frequently. Remove the toasted spices from the pan and set them aside. Place 1 cup water in a saucepan and bring it to a simmer. Remove the saucepan from heat and stir in 2 cups honey. Add the toasted spices and steep for 20 minutes. Strain the syrup and let it cool completely before using or storing.

LIQUEURS & OTHER SPIRITS

Throughout the history of making cocktails, liqueurs were little more than sidekicks, supporting players, there to help the principals look their best. They were invaluable, essential, but seen as not being versatile or deep enough to carry the weight for an entire cocktail. They were one-note, capable of being additive, but incapable of occupying a prominent place.

But, as with a Neil Young guitar solo or Mariano Rivera's cutter, sometimes we discover that a pony with one trick, if it is deployed expertly, prove to be indomitable. There is something appealing about a cocktail that boldly leads with the effortless complexity of an amaro, the spicy, bitter citrus of Campari, or the vegetal, herbaceous, and tobacco flavors present in Chartreuse, a fearlessness that appeals to our minds and tests the tastebuds in unexpected and delightful ways.

In their quest to push the drinks world into new areas, the practitioners in the craft cocktail movement have decided to push their attachment to certain accents to the limit, carefully constructing drinks around their inimitable characters. Not every drink built around these spirits will be for everyone, but there is guaranteed to be at least one drink here for anyone.

One benefit of a drink built around liqueurs and other off-the-well-worn-path spirits is that they cause us to pause where we would otherwise breeze past, cause us to take a moment and appreciate some aspect that had always been hidden away, crowded out by some other element. In a way, they allow us to love what we love in a deeper, fuller manner.

So, whatever your favorite occupant of the "second-tier" is, start thinking about ways to elevate it to the fore, and celebrate it in full.

GLASSWARE: Rocks glass

GARNISH: Shiso leaf, Umeboshi Powder (see recipe)

FARM & VINE

A globe-trotting cocktail that will make you feel right at home.

---

1 oz. aquavit

¾ oz. manzanilla sherry

½ oz. verjus

¾ oz. fresh lime juice

¾ oz. Sugar Snap Pea Syrup (see recipe)

½ oz. egg white

1 oz. Q elderflower tonic

---

1. Place all of the ingredients, except for the elderflower tonic, in a cocktail shaker and dry shake for 10 seconds.

2. Fill the cocktail shaker two-thirds of the way with ice and shake vigorously until chilled.

3. Add the elderflower tonic to the cocktail shaker, strain the cocktail into the rocks glass, and add a few ice cubes.

4. Garnish the cocktail with the shiso leaf and Umeboshi Powder and enjoy.

UMEBOSHI POWDER: Using a dehydrator on a setting for vegetables, spread pitted and pickled umeboshi plums on a tray and dehydrate for 3 days. This will produce a perfectly dry plum, which can then be ground into a powder.

SUGAR SNAP PEA SYRUP: Place ½ cup water in a saucepan and bring it to a boil. Add 1 lb. sugar and stir until it has dissolved. Remove the pan from heat and let the syrup cool. Stir in 5⅓ oz. sugar snap pea juice and use immediately or store in the refrigerator.

GLASSWARE: Coupe

GARNISH: Mace tincture

MACE

An elegant serve courtesy of the team at New York's Mace, Nico de Soto and Greg Boehm.

---

1 oz. Linie aquavit

1 oz. Aperol

½ oz. fresh orange juice

½ oz. freshly pressed beet juice

¾ oz. syrup from can of Lucia young coconut

---

1. Place all of the ingredients in a cocktail shaker, fill it two-thirds of the way with ice, and shake vigorously until chilled.

2. Double strain into the coupe, place the mace tincture in an atomizer, spritz the cocktail with it, and enjoy.

Q & A WITH GREG BOEHM

Greg Boehm is the owner of Cocktail Kingdom and several acclaimed New York City bars, such as Mace. He's had his finger on the pulse of contemporary cocktail culture for more than two decades, and his deep appreciation for the history of cocktails is a big part of the reason why.

Can you tell us a bit about yourself and how you got into the industry?

Sterling, my family's publishing company, published *Classic Cocktails* by Salvatore Calabrese in 1997. At that time I would be in London fairly often and I spent many of those nights at the Library Bar where Salvatore's team would make amazing cocktails. I was hooked, and I started collecting antique cocktail books as my interest in cocktails grew. A couple years later I started importing high-quality barware, and finally started designing and manufacturing barware.

What can you tell us about the creation of Cocktail Kingdom?

Cocktail Kingdom started when I published very accurate facsimile reproductions of some of the most important cocktail books from the 1800s and early 1900s. As I came to know many great bartenders, I was asked to import barware from Japan and Germany, which I did. After talking with many of the top bartenders, I realized there was an opportunity to design and sell barware both based on antiques and more modern styles. Today, Cocktail Kingdom sells barware and glassware to more than 60 countries. We have special barware lines with many of the industry greats, such as David Wondrich, Jeff "Beachbum" Berry, Jeffrey Morgenthaler, Gaz Regan, and Dale DeGroff.

What are the themes of your bars?

Boilermaker is my oldest bar. I wanted to create a place that was more of a "local" that could also make great cocktails. It is the kind of bar that gets better with age. I was actually happy when the banquettes started to get beat up a little. Mace was the next bar that I opened. Nico de Soto was one of my absolute favorite bartenders. The cocktails he made were so good. So he and I decided to open a small bar with spice-focused cocktails. Since Nico and I travel so extensively, and spices are truly international, it was a good fit. The walls are decorated with jars of spices that I carried back from places like Madagascar and India. Next up was Existing Conditions. Don Lee and I had worked together at Cocktail Kingdom for a few years, and we had often discussed opening a bar together. When Don asked if I would want to include Dave Arnold in the mix, I jumped at the chance. We now have a relaxed bar that uses technology and a bit of science to offer a unique cocktail program.

What do you and your team look for when starting a new bar?

I just go with gut instinct when deciding to open a new bar. I do not even put together a business plan. It is all about team building for me. Of course, finding the right space for the right price is important, too.

LAVENDER DREAMS

Though not as popular with bartenders as St-Germain, which works so well in cocktails that it is sometimes called "bartender's ketchup," Giffard's elderflower offering is a little less sweet and syrup, allowing the floral element to come through with a bit more clarity.

½ oz. Giffard wild elderflower liqueur

½ oz. Loch & Union American dry gin

½ oz. Strawberry Syrup (see recipe)

½ oz. fresh lemon juice

Lavender Bubbles (see recipe)

---

1. Place all of the ingredients, except for the Lavender Bubbles, in a cocktail shaker, fill it two-thirds of the way with ice, and shake vigorously until chilled.

2. Double strain into the coupe and spoon the Lavender Bubbles over the top.

STRAWBERRY SYRUP: Place 1½ cups chopped strawberries in a saucepan and cook over low heat until they are soft. Muddle the cooked strawberries, add 1 cup sugar and 1 cup water, and bring to a boil. Remove the pan from heat, cover the pan, and let it rest for 15 minutes. After 15 minutes, place the pan in an ice bath until the mixture is cool. Strain before using or storing.

LAVENDER BUBBLES: Place 5 tablespoons sugar, 1 cup water, and 1 teaspoon dried lavender in a saucepan and bring to a boil, stirring to dissolve the sugar. Remove the pan from heat, cover the pan, and let it rest for 15 minutes. Place the pan in an ice bath until the mixture is cool. Strain, weigh out 14 oz. of liquid, and add to it 2 grams of xanthan gum and 2.5 grams of Versawhip. Use an immersion blender to incorporate them and then use a handheld milk frother to create the bubbles.

GLASSWARE: Champagne flute

GARNISH: Finely grated coconut

EMULS

Some shochu producers bottle the "heads" of their distillation, the first part that distillers usually discard. Called hanatare, it is potent and intense. Washing it with brown butter helps it, and you, take the edge off.

Finely grated coconut, for the rim

1⅓ oz. Brown Butter–Washed Hanatare (see recipe)

½ oz. fresh lemon juice

⅛ oz. pineapple juice

1 bar spoon Orgeat (see page 57)

½ bar spoon white sesame oil

---

1. Wet the rim of the champagne flute and coat it with coconut.

2. Place all of the remaining ingredients in a cocktail shaker and emulsify them with an immersion blender.

3. Double strain the cocktail into the champagne flute and enjoy.

BROWN BUTTER–WASHED HANATARE: Place 5⅓ oz. unsalted butter in a saucepan and melt it over medium heat. Remove the pan from heat, add a 750 ml bottle of hanatare brown sugar shochu, and gently stir to combine. Let the mixture steep for 2 hours. Strain the fat-washed shochu through a coffee filter before using or storing in the refrigerator.

GLASSWARE: Coupe

GARNISH: Edible pink glitter

ROSE BLOSSOM

Don't be fooled by the pink glitter; there's a lot of depth here. The gin imparts a little punch; the Italicus brings earthy, herbal goodness; the elderflower cordial adds something fragrant, and the sparkling wine makes it really refreshing.

---

2 teaspoons Tanqueray No. Ten gin

1¼ oz. Italicus rosolio di bergamotto liqueur

2 teaspoons Bottlegreen elderflower cordial

3 dashes of Peychaud's bitters

Sparkling wine, to top

---

1. Chill the coupe in the freezer.

2. Place all of the ingredients, except for the sparkling wine, in a mixing glass, fill it two-thirds of the way with ice, and stir until chilled.

3. Place a small block of ice in the chilled coupe and double strain the cocktail over it.

4. Top with the sparkling wine, garnish with the edible pink glitter, and enjoy.

GLASSWARE: Mugs

GARNISH: None

THE TOP OF OLYMPUS

A lovely winter warmer that you can take along for a walk in the woods, or sit beside the fireplace with, feeling grateful you're sheltered from the harsh outdoors. These amounts will give you 4 servings.

6 oz. metaxa

10 oz. Spiced Tea Cordial (see recipe)

½ oz. yogurt powder

1. Place all of the ingredients in an appropriately sized container and gently shake it until the yogurt powder has been incorporated.

2. Pour into mugs and enjoy.

SPICED TEA CORDIAL: Place 35 oz. boiling water, 7 oz. sugar, and 10 bags of English breakfast tea in a large mason jar and steep for 2 minutes, stirring gently a few times. Remove the tea bags, place the tea in a saucepan, and add 10 star anise pods, 15 whole cloves, 3 cinnamon sticks, and 2 tablespoons unsalted butter. Warm the mixture over low heat until the flavor is to your liking, 30 to 35 minutes. Strain before using or storing.

TRINIDAD SOUR

Yes, that's a lot of bitters. But placed alongside the Orgeat and lemon juice, the herbaceous punch one would expect is instead translated into one of the most intriguing and complex cocktails on the scene today.

1½ oz. Angostura bitters

½ oz. rye whiskey

¾ oz. fresh lemon juice

1 oz. Orgeat (see page 57)

---

1. Chill the coupe in the freezer.

2. Place all of the ingredients in a cocktail shaker, fill it two-thirds of the way with ice, and shake vigorously until chilled.

3. Strain into the chilled coupe and enjoy.

BITTERS

The recent cocktail renaissance has lifted bitters from a small village where Angostura and Peychaud's were the only inhabitants to a metropolis filled with bespoke alloys and individuals who treat these mysterious tonics with special reverence.

This level of devotion may seem like a bit much, but, considering where bitters originated, it is actually quite fitting. Bitters were initially curatives produced by the European monks that were charged with treating illness before medicine was established as a field. They created their remedies out of herbs, roots, barks, flowers, and spices, producing a series of potions that proved effective enough to be handed down through the centuries. When apothecaries took over the task of providing the public with nostrums, an extremely interesting discovery was made by those who mixed bitters with liquor in order to get the medicine to go down easier: the bitters also worked as a salve for the spirits, taking the bite out of the booze and highlighting its tasty qualities.

It should come as no surprise, then, that the stalwarts of the bitters world, Angostura and Peychaud's, were both the work of medicine men.

Angostura, which Johann G. B. Siegert created while serving as Simón Bolívar's surgeon general, contains over 40 ingredients, though the actual recipe is known by only five people on Earth at any time, and those five take their duty so seriously that they have agreed to never fly on a plane together, knowing that the formula for Angostura would be lost forever in the event of a crash.

Peychaud's was created by a New Orleans pharmacist named Antoine Amédée Peychaud, who liked the effect his family's bitters recipe had on various spirits. Peychaud sold his bitters around town, and when the Merchant's Exchange House mixed them with Cognac and absinthe, the resulting drink, the Sazerac, was such a hit that by the 1890s it was being bottled and sold around the United States.

The role of Angostura and Peychaud's in the cocktail world is similar to the one salt plays in food—a small amount provides balance and accentuates each element so that its full weight can be felt. When adding bitters to a cocktail, act as you would while adding something spicy or pungent to a dish, remaining mindful that you can always add more, but it's impossible to remove once it's in there.

As drinks become more complex and feature increasingly unorthodox ingredients, mixologists have started to explore the long-neglected world of bitters in search of tinctures that go beyond what Angostura and Peychaud's offer. If you're interested in seeing what else is out there, give the offerings from Fee Brothers, Bittermens, Dr. Adam Elmegirab, and Bittercube a look.

GLASSWARE: Rocks glass

GARNISH: Apple blossom

NEWTON PUNCH

Though the story of Issac Newton and the apple is apocryphal, this apple-centric recipe is a fitting homage to his revolutionary discovery of gravity.

---

1 oz. 30 & 40 double jus aperitif de Normandie

1 oz. Somerset cider brandy

1 oz. Briottet manzana verde liqueur

1 oz. Apple & Tea Cordial (see recipe)

1 oz. Curious apple cider

1 oz. fresh lemon juice

1 oz. unfiltered apple juice

---

1. Place all of the ingredients in a mixing glass, fill it two-thirds of the way with ice, and, using another mixing glass, pour the cocktail back and forth between the glasses three times; the more distance between your glasses, the better. This method of mixing is known as the Cuban roll.

2. Strain over a large ice cube into the rocks glass, garnish with the apple blossom, and enjoy.

APPLE & TEA CORDIAL: Place 14 oz. apple juice, 7 oz. brewed Earl Grey tea, and 28 oz. sugar in a saucepan and bring to a boil. Reduce the heat to low and simmer, stirring until the sugar has dissolved. Stir in ⅜ oz. citric acid, remove the pan from heat, and let the mixture cool completely before using or storing.

GLASSWARE: Highball glass
GARNISH: Smoked paprika

A BALCONY IN CHIBA

Subtle and satisfying, this long, refreshing drink also packs quite a punch.

1⅜ oz. shochu

¾ oz. Suntory toki whisky

1 oz. Passion Fruit Cordial (see recipe)

1 egg white

½ oz. fresh lime juice

½ oz. fresh lemon juice

---

1. Place all of the ingredients in a cocktail shaker containing no ice and dry shake for 15 seconds.

2. Fill the cocktail shaker two-thirds of the way with ice and shake vigorously until chilled.

3. Strain over ice into the highball glass, garnish with the paprika, and enjoy.

PASSION FRUIT CORDIAL: Place 17½ oz. passion fruit puree, 3½ oz. fructose, and 7 oz. caster (superfine) sugar in a mason jar and stir until the fructose and sugar have dissolved. Use immediately or store in the refrigerator.

AME SOEUR

A cocktail that shows Camille Cavan's (see pages 328–329) incredible talent for constructing cocktails that are accessible, whimsical, and complex.

1¼ oz. cold-brew coffee

1 oz. Green Chartreuse

1 oz. coconut milk

¾ oz. Simple Syrup (see page 26)

¾ oz. Amaro Dell'Etna

Heavy Vanilla Cream (see recipe), to top

---

1. Place all of the ingredients, except for the vanilla cream, in a cocktail shaker, fill it two-thirds of the way with ice, and shake vigorously until chilled.

2. Double strain into the cocktail glass and layer vanilla cream on top, pouring it slowly over the back of a spoon.

3. Garnish with the edible flower and enjoy.

HEAVY VANILLA CREAM: Place 1 cup heavy whipping cream, 1 oz. vanilla bean paste, and ½ cup Simple Syrup and shake vigorously until the cream is very thick. Use immediately or store in the refrigerator.

GLASSWARE: Coupe

GARNISH: None

POTATO STOCKING

This clever riff on the Silk Stocking calls for sweet potato shochu where the tequila usually goes, and amazake in place of the cream. The result is just as smooth as its inspiration, but with a more pleasant bite.

---

1 oz. sweet potato shochu

¾ oz. white crème de cacao

⅓ oz. amazake

Dash of Luxardo maraschino liqueur

---

1. Place all of the ingredients in a cocktail shaker, fill it two-thirds of the way with ice, and shake vigorously until chilled.

2. Double strain into the coupe and enjoy.

Q & A WITH CAMILLE CAVAN

After resisting the call for years, Camille Cavan eventually accepted her considerable talents behind the bar. With a unique perspective and flair for simple, complex, and playful cocktails, Cavan is a major reason that Portland's cocktail scene is one of America's best.

How did you get interested in cocktails?

I worked in one of the first craft cocktail spots in Portland years ago, while working part-time in the music industry, and found the cocktails to be inspiring, elevated, and created with thought and care. I hadn't really seen cocktails to be that elevated before. After that bar closed, I moved to another restaurant where I began playing with cocktail creations and was surprised by how easy flavor profiles, vision, and intuition with what would work came to me. Ironically, I pushed back from being a creator of cocktails, almost saying to myself, "I don't want to be great at this," but eventually gave in to this calling.

Who has influenced you in terms of cocktails?

I worked underneath Jeffrey Morgenthaler in Eugene, before he moved to Portland, and I was able to get a glimpse into true hospitality. Aaron Zieske, now of Scotch Lodge, first showed me the care that comes with elevated cocktails and I saw how intimate that could be. However, I find myself to be extremely self-taught, pushing through barriers and boundaries.

Any favorite stories from your time behind the bar?

There's really nothing better than having a guest order a cocktail, watch you make it, and then watch the joy come over them and get genuinely happy, and their time becomes better because of it. Or if a guest goes out of their way to come and tell you that the cocktail you made them was the best cocktail of their life. That type of story beats any other story, like someone famous coming in or a crazy moment with a guest—there's no better feeling.

What's your favorite cocktail to make?

It varies and changes often. People do not realize how often their palate shifts, how they may really enjoy something they haven't in the past, so I love to make cocktails that someone may not think they want but ultimately end up really making an impression, like a rum Old Fashioned or a tropical rum-based cocktail with coconut milk.

However, my all-time favorite cocktail to make is a Pisco Sour. I love the heavy citrus elements, the rustic earthiness of the pisco, and I am a sucker for egg white—anything that's frothy is my jam. I do not trust shaken cocktails that do not have any head.

What is essential for novice cocktail makers to have in their home bar?

The makings for a mezcal Negroni . . . but with coffee. Coffee bitters, coffee liqueur, cold brew, whatever works for you.

What is your process for creating cocktails?

I have a very different approach than many. I always think of flavors, profiles, and liquors I haven't used or visited in a while then begin putting combination ideas on paper. I could be waiting in line at the grocery store, on a walk, or making dinner and I will stop and make a note on my phone. I then go to work, and put these flavors together, tweak them, and they either may not be exactly what I had envisioned—in which case I stop the process and discard the idea, because rarely do good cocktails happen when they're forced—or they're gems and going on the menu the next day. I work fast and impulsively, oftentimes creating a cocktail the day I put it on the menu. I also never do whole cocktail menu re-vamps, especially as the sole creator of the cocktail program.

Is there an absolute no-no in cocktail making?

Do not shake straight spirits. Adding more ingredients will not fix a cocktail. Cocktail creation is not about you, it's not an ego trip or something that is for your palate. A good creator thinks about the guest; the varieties of different tastes, what will make them happy and feel taken care of. Lastly, do not take things personally.

What makes a cocktail into a craft cocktail?

The type of ingredients chosen; the care taken for those ingredients; correct execution for each cocktail. This includes ice, dilution, and choosing combinations that highlight each ingredient.

A NIGHT IN TUNISIA

The national liqueur of the Czech Republic, Becherovka's complex mix of herbs and spices makes it a fantastic cocktail ingredient, one that the ambitious mixologist would be wise to experiment liberally with.

---

1 oz. Hoshiko umeshu

1 oz. Becherovka

½ oz. fresh lemon juice

1 egg white

Dash of Bob's liquorice bitters

---

1. Place all of the ingredients in a cocktail shaker, fill it two-thirds of the way with ice, and shake vigorously until chilled.

2. Strain into the coupe and enjoy.

DANCE OF TWINKLE & SHADOW

Gyokuro tea, which is both sweet and savory, provides a stage for the absinthe to work its magic.

---

2 bar spoons loose-leaf gyokuro tea

2 oz. hot water

1 oz. absinthe

---

1. Place the tea in a teapot and add the hot water and absinthe. Steep for 2 minutes.

2. Pour over an ice cube into the ceramic bowl, garnish with the salted cherry blossom, and enjoy.

GLASSWARE: Coupe

GARNISH: Matcha-dusted warabi mochi

SHINZO NO TOBIRA

This cocktail reverses the Japanese custom of serving green tea with wagashi confectionery, putting the wagashi flavors in the drink and the green tea on the side with the matcha-dusted mochi.

1½ oz. Japanese Mix (see recipe)

½ oz. Mugwort Shochu (see recipe)

½ oz. water

1 bar spoon wasanbon sugar

Spritz of 25 Percent Saline Solution (see page 166)

---

1. Place all of the ingredients, except for the saline solution, in a mixing glass, fill it two-thirds of the way with ice, and stir until chilled.

2. Strain into the coupe and spritz with the saline solution.

3. Garnish with the matcha-dusted warabi mochi and enjoy.

JAPANESE MIX: Place 2 cups soy milk and 1 teaspoon agar agar powder in a saucepan and warm it over medium heat, stirring to dissolve the powder. Add another 2 cups soy milk, 4 cups SG Kome shochu, ¾ cup kinako (roasted soy flour), and 1⅔ cups molasses and stir to combine. Remove the pan from heat and chill the mixture in the refrigerator for 12 hours. Strain through cheesecloth before using or storing.

MUGWORT SHOCHU: Place ⅓ oz. dry mugwort and a 750 ml bottle of SG Kome shochu in a large mason jar and steep for 24 hours at room temperature. Strain before using or storing.

GLASSWARE: Rocks glass

GARNISH: Pandan leaf

LEEWARD NEGRONI

The coconut and pandan manage to bring the best out of one of the world's great liqueurs, Campari.

Bittermens 'Elemakule Tiki Bitters, to rinse

1 oz. Coconut Oil–Washed Campari (see recipe)

¾ oz. Pandan Cordial (see recipe)

½ oz. Sipsmith V.J.O.P. gin

---

1. Rinse a rocks glass with the bitters then discard the bitters.

2. Place the remaining ingredients in a mixing glass, fill it two-thirds of the way with ice, and stir until chilled.

3. Strain over a large ice cube into the rocks glass, garnish with the pandan leaf, and enjoy.

COCONUT OIL–WASHED CAMPARI: Place 2 cups virgin coconut oil and 4 cups Campari in a large mason jar and let it sit at room temperature for 24 hours, stirring occasionally. Place the mixture in the freezer overnight. Remove the solidified layer of fat and strain the Campari through a coffee filter before using or storing.

PANDAN CORDIAL: Place 10 sliced pandan leaves and 4 cups Everclear in a large mason jar and steep for 48 hours. Strain and add 1½ cups Simple Syrup (see page 26) for every 1 cup of tincture.

GLASSWARE: Snifter

GARNISH: None

CHARTREUSE SLUSHY

A playful vehicle for the serious depth that resides within Green Chartreuse.

2¼ oz. tart lemonade

1 oz. Green Chartreuse

2½ oz. Rich Simple Syrup (see page 59)

---

1. Place all of the ingredients in a blender, add 4 oz. crushed ice, and puree until smooth.

2. Pour the drink into the snifter and enjoy.

A sole French element amidst a host of Italian ingredients, the Lillet proves to be a quick study here.

---

1 oz. Cynar 70

1 oz. Punt e Mes sweet vermouth

¾ oz. Cucumber-Infused Campari (see recipe)

½ oz. Lillet

¼ oz. Luxardo maraschino cherry liqueur

---

1. Place all of the ingredients in a mixing glass, fill it two-thirds of the way with ice, and stir until chilled.

2. Place a large ice cube in the rocks glass, strain the cocktail over it, garnish with the strip of orange peel, and enjoy.

CUCUMBER-INFUSED CAMPARI: Peel and chop 1 large cucumber and place it in a large mason jar. Add 4 cups Campari and steep in a cool, dark place for 1 week. Strain before using or storing.

CHARTREUSE SWIZZLE

The most iconic 21st century cocktail from one of the centers of the modern cocktail revolution, San Francisco.

1½ oz. Green Chartreuse

1 oz. pineapple juice

¾ oz. fresh lime juice

½ oz. John D. Taylor's velvet falernum

---

1. Fill the swizzle glass with pebble ice, add all of the ingredients, and use the swizzle method to combine: place a swizzle stick between your hands, lower the swizzle stick into the drink, and quickly rub your palms together to rotate the stick as you move it up and down in the drink. When frost begins to form on the outside of the glass, the drink is ready.

2. Top with more pebble ice if desired and enjoy.

RED TEMPLES

Shochu provides a calm beginning for what becomes a wild yet elegant ride full of fruit, bitter, nuttiness, floral notes, and smoke.

1 strawberry

1 oz. Iichiko Saiten shochu

¾ oz. Campari

¾ oz. Amontillado sherry

¼ oz. St-Germain

5 dashes of peaty Scotch whisky

1. Place the strawberry in a mixing glass and muddle.

2. Add the remaining ingredients and ice and stir until chilled.

3. Double strain over ice into the rocks glass, garnish with the torched cinnamon stick and maraschino cherries, and enjoy.

GLASSWARE: Copper cup or wineglass
GARNISH: None

NEGRONI CARBONATO

An update on the Negroni Sbagliato that is certain to turn heads.

1½ oz. Campari

1 oz. Byrrh grand quinquina

½ oz. Cynar

½ oz. verjus

¼ oz. lemon sorbet

1½ oz. Cava

½ oz. Perrier

Dash of orange bitters

1 orange peel

---

1. Place all of the ingredients in a 6 oz. bottle and carbonate it, using a SodaStream or a similar device. Cap the bottle immediately, do not shake or stir, and store in the refrigerator overnight.

2. Pour over crushed ice into the copper cup and enjoy.

FLIRTBIRD

This take on the Jungle Bird, a tiki classic, makes artful use of Japanese ingredients.

Plum powder, for the rim

1 shiso leaf

1½ oz. shochu

1 oz. fresh yuzu juice

½ oz. agave nectar

---

1. Wet the rim of the cup and coat it with the plum powder.

2. Tear the shiso leaf in half and add to shaker with the remaining ingredients. Fill the shaker two-thirds of the way with ice and shake vigorously until chilled.

3. Strain over a large ice cube into the cup, garnish with the shiso leaf, and enjoy.

GLASSWARE: Footed pilsner glass

GARNISH: Fresh mint sprig, edible flower, cocktail umbrella

VOODOO CHILD

Infusing the candied citrus and spice of falernum with the creamy character of cashews makes for a spellbinding concoction.

---

2 tablespoons popping passion fruit boba

1 oz. fresh lemon juice

½ oz. Cashew-Infused Falernum (see recipe)

½ oz. Orgeat (see page 57)

---

1. Place the popping passion fruit boba in the pilsner glass.

2. Place the remaining ingredients in a cocktail shaker, fill it two-thirds of the way with ice, and shake vigorously until chilled.

3. Fill the pilsner glass with ice and strain the cocktail over it.

4. Garnish with the fresh mint, edible flower, and cocktail umbrella and enjoy.

CASHEW-INFUSED FALERNUM: Place 1 cup cashews in a skillet and toast until lightly browned, shaking the skillet occasionally. Place 4 cups John D. Taylor's Falernum in a large mason jar, add the toasted cashews, and steep for 48 hours. Strain before using or storing.

GLASSWARE: Rocks glass

GARNISH: Edible flowers, matcha powder

SPRING IN TOKYO

Umeshu is the result of steeping ume plums in shochu, and its sweet, slightly tangy flavor fills in the gaps between the shochu and the yuzu in this drink.

¾ oz. Mizu lemongrass shochu

¾ oz. umeshu

½ oz. fresh yuzu juice

½ oz. Simple Syrup (see page 26)

½ oz. egg white

1. Place all of the ingredients in a cocktail shaker, fill it two-thirds of the way with ice, and shake vigorously until chilled.

2. Strain the cocktail into a glass, discard the ice, and return the cocktail to the shaker. Dry shake for 10 seconds.

3. Strain over an ice sphere into the rocks glass, garnish with the edible flowers and matcha powder, and enjoy.

KARAJUKU GIMLET

The delicately floral Kaffir Lime Cordial and green tea–infused shochu make for a gorgeously simple and delightful cocktail.

1½ oz. Green Tea–Infused Shochu (see recipe)

¾ oz. Kaffir Lime Cordial (see recipe)

---

1. Place all of the ingredients in a mixing glass, fill it two-thirds of the way with ice, and stir until chilled.

2. Strain into the tea cup, garnish with the lime leaves, and enjoy.

GREEN TEA–INFUSED SHOCHU: Place a 750 ml bottle of Mizu lemongrass shochu and 1 oz. loose-leaf green tea in a large mason jar and steep for 8 minutes. Strain before using or storing.

KAFFIR LIME CORDIAL: Place 4 cups water, 1¼ cups sugar, 2 teaspoons tartaric acid, 1 teaspoon malic acid, and a dash of citric acid in a saucepan and cook over medium heat until the mixture is well combined. Remove the pan from heat and let the cordial cool before using or storing.

GLASSWARE: Brandy snifter

GARNISH: Orange twist

GO AHEAD ROMEO

Aperol almost glows when it's frozen, and as it starts to melt its citrus notes add another layer to the cocktail. Don't hesitate to try these ice cubes in other cocktails as well.

---

6 Aperol Ice Cubes (see recipe)

4 oz. Prosecco

---

1. Place Aperol Ice Cubes in the snifter and pour the Prosecco over them.

2. Garnish with the orange twist and enjoy.

APEROL ICE CUBES: Combine ¼ cup Aperol and ¾ cup water, pour the mixture into ice cube trays, and freeze until solid.

GLASSWARE: Rocks glass

GARNISH: Edible gold leaf

TAIKOH

Three auspicious Japanese ingredients—matcha, sake, and gold leaf—team to form something light, sweet, bitter, and delicately tart.

1⅓ oz. sake

¾ oz. green tea liqueur

1 bar spoon matcha powder

2 bar spoons fresh sudachi or lime juice

---

1. Place all of the ingredients in a cocktail shaker, fill it two-thirds of the way with ice, and shake vigorously until chilled.

2. Strain over ice into the rocks glass, garnish with the edible gold leaf, and enjoy.

TRENCH 75

Nikka Coffey gin is more citrus-y than juniper-forward, which means it plays a little bit nicer with others. Here, it provides an opportunity for the sparkling sake to shine.

---

1 oz. Nikka Coffey gin

½ oz. fresh lemon juice

2 bar spoons Honey Syrup (see page 80)

1 oz. Shichiken sparkling sake

---

1. Place the gin, lemon juice, and syrup in a cocktail shaker, fill it two-thirds of the way with ice, and shake vigorously until chilled.

2. Strain into the coupe and top with the sparkling sake.

3. Garnish with the dehydrated lime wheel and enjoy.

GLASSWARE: Footed pilsner glass

GARNISH: Lemon wheel, lime wheel, apple slices, fresh mint

PROPER CUP

Ginger beer and a vanilla-spiked Apple Syrup add an air of refinement to the Pimm's Cup, while maintaining its accessible nature.

---

2 cucumber ribbons

2 oz. Pimm's

¾ oz. Hendrick's gin

Dash of Angostura bitters

2 dashes of Peychaud's bitters

½ oz. fresh lemon juice

½ oz. fresh lime juice

1 oz. Apple Syrup (see recipe)

Ginger beer, to top

---

1. Place the cucumber ribbons in the footed pilsner glass.

2. Place all of the remaining ingredients, except for the ginger beer, in a cocktail shaker, fill it two-thirds of the way with ice, and shake vigorously 20 times.

3. Strain into the glass and top with ginger beer.

4. Garnish with the lemon wheel, lime wheel, apple slices, and fresh mint and enjoy.

APPLE SYRUP: Slice an apple and place it in a medium saucepan with 1 cup water, 1 cup sugar, and ½ teaspoon pure vanilla extract. Bring to a boil over medium heat, reduce the heat to medium-low, and simmer for 5 minutes. Remove the pan from heat and let the syrup cool completely. Strain before using or storing.

GLASSWARE: Cocktail glass

GARNISH: Green cocktail cherry

ETRENNE

A cocktail that looks as vibrant as it tastes. For green banana liqueur, Pisang Ambon and Bols are strong options.

½ oz. vodka

⅔ oz. green banana liqueur

2 bar spoons mint liqueur

½ oz. heavy cream

---

1. Place all of the ingredients in a cocktail shaker, fill it two-thirds of the way with ice, and shake vigorously until chilled.

2. Double strain into the cocktail glass, garnish with the green cocktail cherry, and enjoy.

GLASSWARE: Coupe
GARNISH: None

I WILL SURVIVE

Chartreuse helps punch up the natural vegetal qualities present in this twist on the Bloody Mary. As you can guess from the name, this is the drink of choice when you feel like life, or your hangover, is grinding you down.

---

1 teaspoon chipotle chile powder, for the rim

1 teaspoon kosher salt, for the rim, plus more to taste

1 oz. Green Chartreuse

1 oz. fresh lime juice

2½ oz. tomato juice

3 dashes of Worcestershire sauce

3 dashes of Tabasco chipotle sauce

Black pepper, to taste

2 dashes of celery bitters

---

1. Chill the coupe in the freezer.

2. Place the chipotle powder and the salt in a saucer and stir to combine. Wet the rim of the coupette and dip it into the mixture.

3. Add the remaining ingredients to the glass, stir to combine, and enjoy.

GLASSWARE: Coupe

GARNISH: Freshly grated nutmeg

BOLIVAR SOUR

The nutmeg garnish helps accentuate the richness provided by the Orgeat.

⅞ oz. Angostura bitters

⅞ oz. Mount Gay eclipse rum

¾ oz. Orgeat (see page 57)

⅞ oz. fresh lime juice

---

1. Place all of the ingredients in a cocktail shaker, fill it two-thirds of the way with ice, and shake vigorously until chilled.

2. Strain into the coupe, grate the nutmeg over the cocktail for a garnish, and enjoy.

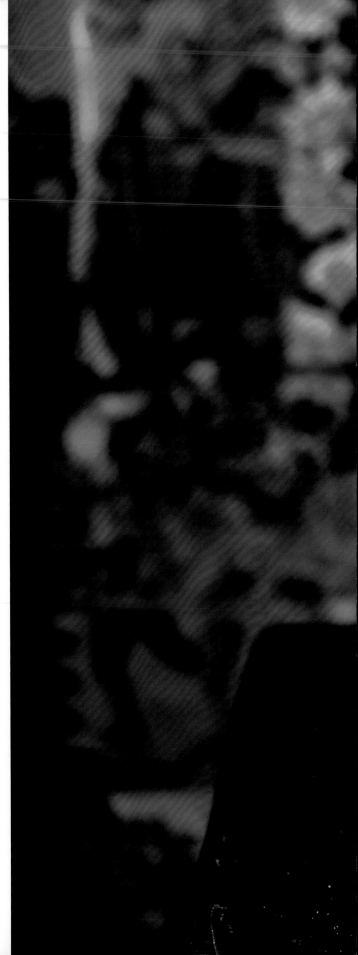

GLASSWARE: Chilled rocks glass
GARNISH: Strip of lemon peel, brandied cherry

AMARETTO SOUR

Jeffrey Morgenthaler, who is widely regarded as one of the best bartenders in America, swears he makes the best Amaretto Sour in the world. His secret? Using cask-proof bourbon and an immersion blender prior to shaking to ensure that the egg whites get extra fluffy.

1½ oz. Amaretto

¾ oz. cask-proof bourbon

1 oz. fresh lemon juice

1 teaspoon Rich Simple Syrup (see page 59)

½ oz. fresh egg white

---

1. Chill the rocks glass in the freezer.

2. Place all of the ingredients in a cocktail shaker and dry shake for 10 seconds.

3. Add ice to the shaker and shake vigorously until chilled.

4. Strain over ice into the chilled rocks glass, garnish with the lemon peel and brandied cherry, and enjoy.

Q & A WITH JEFFREY MORGENTHALER

In Portland, the name Jeffrey Morgenthaler is inextri-
cably linked with cocktails. He has a way of creating
unique, yet familiar cocktails and did so for years
while working at Clyde Commons.

**How did you become interested in cocktails? How did
you get started?**

How did I get started? Well, I went to architecture
school at the University of Oregon in the 1990s, and I
needed a summer job, back in 1996. I went to the career center and there weren't a ton of paying architecture jobs because they usually offer internships for
no pay, which was not going to work for me. But I saw
a bartending job, and I'd never tended bar before. I'd
never even spent much time in bars, but I thought it
sounded like a cool job and I applied and got my first
bartending job.

**Besides you, who would you say has influenced the
Portland cocktail scene? And who influenced you?**

Oh, I mean hands down, the most important person
in Portland bartending is Lucy Brennan. She really
brought cocktails to Oregon, and to Portland, was
really the first person to put Portland on a larger
stage for doing something different and unique. She
released a book, I want to say in the early 2000s,
called *Hip Sips*, full of recipes from her establishments, the two establishments that she had, and it
was super influential.

How do you think Portland's cocktail scene has evolved since you started?

When I got here, there was just a small handful of bartenders kind of doing interesting cocktails. Portland hadn't really hit the main stage yet. And during my time here, I was able to watch things blow up. As more people moved here, the city was placed on a national and international stage for culture, and for dining, and for drinking, and wine and beer and stuff, and so nowadays it's hard to get a bad drink because there are so many fantastic bars in Portland.

What do you think makes Portland's bar scene unique?

Oregon in general has sort of been defined by a kind of DIY mentality and that has really been reflected in the cocktail-bar world, especially in the past 15 years or so. People creating, really taking matters into their own hands and creating their own ingredients and creating their own styles and recipes.

What's your favorite cocktail to make, for yourself?

Probably an Old-Fashioned. It's one of the drinks we're most known for at our bar.

What do you think is essential for novice bartenders to have in their home bars?

I always recommend a good shaker and a good strainer. I'm not one to go for super-fancy expensive equipment. I think that it's the craftsman and not the tools. But I think a shaker and a strainer and some sort of way to measure things are indispensable.

There's now an automated cocktail bar in Las Vegas. Do you think bartenders will be rendered obsolete at some point?

Nope. I don't. I think that those automated bar things are probably going to end up being used in Vegas instead of bartenders working behind the scenes making drinks for tables, but they'll never be able to replace the experience of going in and sitting at a bar and talking to a bartender. That's just not how it works.

What's your process for creating cocktails?

My process . . . I mean, it's similar to any design process. I start with a concept and kind of flesh that out as fully as I can, and then I just begin working to try and execute that concept. And there's a fair amount of trial and error in the execution, but once I have a really solid concept, it usually comes together very quickly.

Is there one absolute no-no in cocktail making?

No, not really. I think that being too prescriptive in this kind of stuff is a bad thing. Drink whatever you like.

FLEUR DE LIS

The verjus is the key to keeping the rich combination of Peychaud's and Cognac from overwhelming.

---

1 oz. Peychaud's bitters

¾ oz. Pierre Ferrand ambre Cognac

¾ oz. Montinore verjus

¼ oz. Honey Water (see page 187)

2 lemon peels

Sparkling wine, to top

---

1. Place all of the ingredients, except for the sparkling wine, in a mixing glass, fill it two-thirds of the way with ice, and stir until chilled.

2. Strain over a large ice cube into the rocks glass, top with sparkling wine, and enjoy.

GLASSWARE: Rocks glass

GARNISH: Spritz of Becherovka, strip of orange peel

TETON TANYA

Inspired by the classic Boulevardier cocktail, this drink combines the dry, spice-driven flavor of Cynar with the bright, bittersweet Aperol.

---

1 oz. Aperol

1 oz. Cynar

1 oz. rye whiskey

---

1. Place all of the ingredients in a mixing glass, fill it two-thirds of the way with ice, and stir until chilled.

2. Strain over a large ice cube into the rocks glass, garnish with the spritz of Becherovka and strip of orange peel, and enjoy.

GLASSWARE: Collins glass

GARNISH: None

GOODNIGHT, MOON

An extraordinary cocktail that seems both like some magical potion from the ancient world and on the cutting edge of modern mixology.

---

1 oz. Pommeau de Normandie

½ oz. heavy cream

2½ oz. Fennel & Walnut Syrup (see recipe)

1 oz. club soda

---

1. Add ice to the Collins glass and build the drink in the glass, adding the ingredients in the order they are listed.

2. Stir until chilled and enjoy.

FENNEL & WALNUT SYRUP: Place equal parts maple-walnut syrup and freshly pressed fennel juice in a mason jar, stir well, and use as desired.

WINE, BRANDY, COGNAC & VERMOUTH

These grape-based alcoholic beverages are among the oldest in the world, and so have always been a compelling component in cocktails—from bridging the bold flavors of gin and Campari in a Negroni, as vermouth does, to serving as the foundation of bonafide classics, as Cognac does in a Sidecar and pisco, the aromatic, South American brandy, does in the Pisco Sour.

Part of the appeal is how well grape-based spirits play with others, a quality that comes from a nature that is both malleable and expressive. The former can be seen in both the choices that a winemaker makes during harvesting and the aging process, or how a completed wine can be fortified with another spirit, as it is in vermouth and sherry. Wine's impressive expressiveness is shown through its ability to articulate the terroir, or the elements present during its birth, from the minerals in the soil to the weather conditions during a particular growing season. This ability to communicate also extends to the mixologist who is working with it, allowing them to express intentions that other spirits would stand in the way of.

Another bonus to working with the members of this group: if you do not end up utilizing a wine or grape-based distillate in your final drink, thinking about including them can often open up possibilities that were previously unseen, allowing you to see what flavor is needed to provide both balance and intrigue.

In the end, wine and its family members are familiar enough to everyone that a drink based around them will be agreeable and accessible, no matter how bold the overall conception of the drink is. Working with them allows you to take chances and make an impression without seeming too pushy, an underrated attribute in a space that is always teetering on the edge of prizing the creator over the customer. Think of them as a means to facilitate a genial conversation between the expert and the uninitiated, and you'll end up with cocktails that please a wide spectrum of palates.

The combination of the elderflower liqueur and rose syrup lead the descent into a riotous flowery bouquet.

1¾ oz. Viognier

1 oz. Hendrick's gin

2 teaspoons St-Germain

2 teaspoons Monin rose syrup

1 teaspoon agave nectar

1. Chill the cocktail glass in the freezer.

2. Place all of the ingredients in a mixing glass, fill it two-thirds of the way with ice, and stir until chilled.

3. Strain into the chilled glass, garnish with the dried rosebud, and enjoy.

GLASSWARE: Rocks glass

GARNISH: None

WITCH DOCTOR

Cognac, mezcal, and Cynar team to open your eyes—
particularly the third one.

---

1 fresh sage leaf

¾ oz. Cognac

¾ oz. mezcal

½ oz. Cocchi Vermouth di Torino

¼ oz. Cynar

¼ oz. Luxardo maraschino liqueur

2 dashes of grapefruit bitters

1 strip of grapefruit peel

---

1. Place the sage leaf on a small plate, ignite it, and place
    the rocks glass over it, upside down. Discard the burnt
    sage leaf and add 1 large ice cube to the glass.

2. Place all of the ingredients, except for the strip of grape-
    fruit peel, in a mixing glass, fill it two-thirds of the way
    with ice, and stir until chilled.

3. Strain into the rocks glass, express the strip of grapefruit
    peel over the cocktail, discard the peel, and enjoy.

GLASSWARE: Collins glass

GARNISH: Lemon twist

BLACK GOLD

A sublime deconstruction, breaking a Rum & Coke down to its elements and piecing them back together in a way that is at once recognizable and eye-opening.

Dash of Orinoco bitters

½ teaspoon Fernet-Branca

¾ oz. Burly Cascara cola syrup

1 oz. Bacardi Facundo NEO rum

4 oz. Champagne

---

1. Place all of the ingredients, except for the Champagne, in the Collins glass, add ice, and stir until chilled.

2. Top with the Champagne, garnish with the lemon twist, and enjoy.

GLASSWARE: White wineglass

GARNISH: None

YOKOTA

There's no wasted motion in this cocktail—every element brings something to the table.

---

1 oz. Lustau moscatel sherry

2 bar spoons fresh lemon juice

2 bar spoons Simple Syrup (see page 26)

Cava, to top

---

1. Place all of the ingredients, except for the Cava, in a blender with crushed ice, pulse gently until the mixture is slushy, and pour it into the white wineglass.

2. Top with the Cava, use a spoon to lift it, incorporating it into the slushy, and enjoy.

DECI'S ROOMMATE

The lime juice and Rosé air out the Calvados just enough
make it agreeable.

---

1 oz. Calvados

¾ oz. fresh lime juice

½ oz. Rich Simple Syrup (see page 59)

2 oz. sparkling Rosé

---

1. Place the Calvados, lime juice, and simple syrup in a
   cocktail shaker, fill it two-thirds of the way with ice, an
   shake vigorously until chilled.

2. Pour the Rosé into the shaker and strain over ice into t
   rocks glass.

3. Garnish with the fresh mint and enjoy.

BURNT ORANGE SHERRY COBBLER

Coming up with such a simple tweak to make orange juice work with a Japanese whisky is a stroke of genius.

1½ oz. fino sherry

1 oz. Japanese whisky

1 oz. Burnt Orange Juice (see recipe)

¼ oz. fresh lemon juice

¼ oz. Demerara Syrup (see page 36)

---

1. Add crushed ice to the highball glass. Add all of the ingredients and use the swizzle method to combine: place a swizzle stick between your hands, lower the swizzle stick into the drink, and quickly rub your palms together to rotate the stick as you move it up and down in the drink. When frost begins to form on the outside of the highball glass, the drink is ready.

2. Top with more crushed ice, garnish with the pineapple leaf, edible flower, and cinnamon stick, and enjoy.

BURNT ORANGE JUICE: Prepare a gas or charcoal grill for low heat (350°F). Halve an orange and place it cut side down on the grill. Grill until the sugars start to caramelize and grill marks appear on the orange. Squeeze the juice into a mason jar.

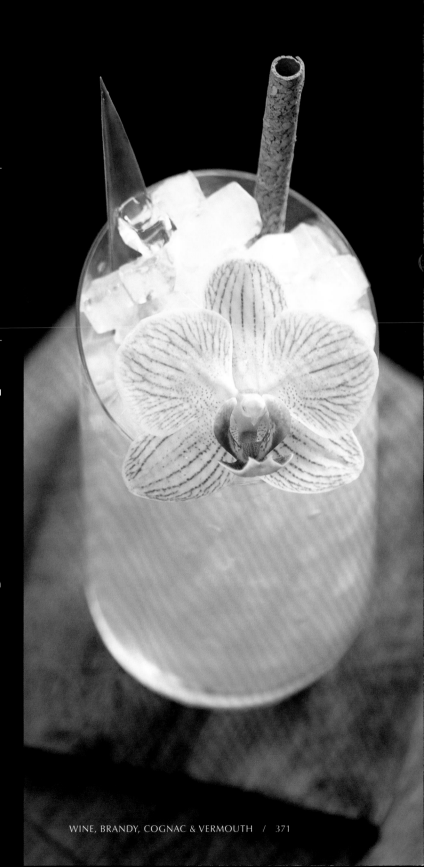

GLASSWARE: Flip cup

GARNISH: Lemon twist

PISCO PUNCH

Just accept the fact that you'll have to improvise the Nichol Juice—reportedly one person in the world knows the recipe. It is known that the key ingredient is kaffir lime leaves, but there are a number of other things in this tincture, which is so named because of Duncan Nichol, who invented the drink in the 19th century.

---

2 oz. pisco

1 oz. fresh lemon juice

¾ oz. Pineapple Syrup (see page 179)

3 to 4 dashes of Nichol Juice

---

1. Place all of the ingredients in a cocktail shaker, fill it two-thirds of the way with ice, and shake vigorously until chilled.

2. Double strain over an ice cube into the flip cup, garnish with the lemon twist, and enjoy.

MODERNIZED MARTINEZ

The high amount of vermouth is not a typo, but an homage—the original, which reaches back more than 100 years, also features a larger amount of vermouth than gin.

1½ oz. sweet vermouth

1 oz. Old Tom gin

1 bar spoon Luxardo maraschino liqueur

Dash of Angostura bitters

2 dashes of orange bitters

---

1. Place all of the ingredients in a mixing glass, fill it two-thirds of the way with ice, and stir until chilled.

2. Strain into the cocktail glass, garnish with the lemon peel, and enjoy.

Glassware: Large tulip glass
Garnish: Toasted black walnuts

FORTUNATO'S REVIVER

A cocktail that looks back to the heyday of the soda fountain for inspiration.

1½ oz. Bodegas Yuste aurora Amontillado sherry

½ oz. Cocchi Vermouth di Torino

½ oz. Demerara Syrup (see page 36)

3½ oz. vanilla ice cream

3½ oz. honey ice cream

3 tablespoons chopped black walnuts, lightly toasted

---

1. Chill the large tulip glass in the freezer.

2. Place all of the ingredients in a blender and puree until smooth.

3. Pour the drink into the chilled glass, garnish with toasted black walnuts, and enjoy.

IN THE PINES, UNDER THE PALMS

Many different worlds combine in this unique masterpiece created by Nicolas Torres at True Laurel, one of the best bar in America, and the world.

¾ oz. Oliveros vermouth

¾ oz. St. George terroir gin

¾ oz. Toasted Coconut Rye (see recipe)

¼ oz. Luxardo maraschino liqueur

¼ oz. water

2 dashes of Angostura bitters

1 redwood or pine sprout

---

1. Place all of the ingredients in a mixing glass, fill it two-thirds of the way with ice, and stir until chilled.

2. Strain over ice into the rocks glass, garnish with a redwood or pine sprout, and enjoy.

TOASTED COCONUT RYE: Place 4 cups rye whiskey in a large mason jar. Place 2 heaping tablespoons organic coconut oil in a saucepan and warm it over medium heat until it gently simmers. Add 1 cup coconut flakes and remove the pan from heat. Stir the flakes until they start to turn brown. Add the coconut mixture to the mason jar while the oil is still in liquid form. Seal the jar, shake it vigorously, and let the mixture sit for 10 minutes. Shake vigorously, place the jar in the freezer, and let it sit overnight. Remove the fat layer and strain the whiskey before using or storing.

Q & A WITH NICOLAS TORRES

Even with the success David Barzelay and Nicolas Torres had after opening the acclaimed restaurant Lazy Bear in San Francisco's Mission District, they decided Torres's gifts as a mixologist needed room to grow.

Enter True Laurel, a cocktail bar imbued with mid-century whimsy—there is a reason the room's design centerpiece is a wall sculpture inspired by Isamu Noguchi's playscapes—that is reflected in a rotating list of cocktails that celebrates the never-ending abundance of local ingredients.

What can you tell us about how the bar was started?

Chef David and I had been working together for about 3 years at Lazy Bear, and we were always looking for ways to improve the bar program. One day we realized that our ideas may have outgrown what we could do within the confines of Lazy Bear, so we searched for a new space that could focus a little more on drinks, but carry a similar ethos.

What is the theme of the bar and its focus?

I don't think we were going for a theme. Our focus is working with seasons and the farmers that supply our stuff. We want to use the most of the bounty California has to offer, and we want to use what we can get to the extent that we hopefully waste as little as possible. There are definitely bars we looked at for flow and back-of-house operations, but as for look and feel we really took our own path, and found it very important to do so.

What do you look for when creating new cocktails?

I usually start with the produce and work backward. I'm typically looking for ways to use good produce, rare wines, and common spirits. This formula has

been good to me. I strive for balance and a certain lightness.

What are the best parts of running a cocktail bar? Are there any downsides or things that make it difficult?

This city is saturated with food and cocktails, it is very gluttonous at times. The hard part is staying competitive. The city is always looking for what's next. It also constantly pushes you as an artist to perform. At the same time, there is so much support in the industry, and we all try to learn from each other.

Blue Hawaiian, Brandy Alexander, Pink Squirrel, Rusty Nail, Tom Collins, White Russian, Grasshopper, Rob Roy, Pink Lady: If you had to pick one of these classic cocktails to add to your cocktail menu how would you make it fit in with your style?

Tom Collins for sure, I still order them all the time. It's a beautiful cocktail. Like a lot of simple sours, or fizz in this case, the details really matter. Simple yet complex, you can learn so much from that drink. It is the base of so many fizzes, coolers, daisies that came after it.

Do you have a personal favorite cocktail?

I'm a huge Highball fan, brandy and soda please.

Do you have a favorite spirit to work with when making cocktails?

I think about wines and fortified wines more than I think about spirits, or at least when I'm trying to use a certain spirit I often think what wine would go well with it.

RED JUBILEE

Chinese five-spice powder may seem like a strange ingredient to incorporate in a cocktail, but its flavor is anise-forward, meaning its right at home.

---

2 oz. Cognac

¾ oz. fresh lemon juice

¾ oz. Simple Syrup (see page 26)

¼ teaspoon Chinese five-spice powder

5 dashes of Peychaud's bitters

---

1. Place all of the ingredients in a cocktail shaker, fill it two-thirds of the way with ice, and shake vigorously until chilled.

2. Strain over ice into the rocks glass, garnish with the star anise pod and maraschino cherry, and enjoy.

GLASSWARE: Cocktail glass
GARNISH: None

LAST DANCE

A cocktail that uncovered one of the universe's eternal truths: Calvados and chestnuts are a dream combination.

⅔ oz. Calvados

½ oz. mint liqueur

½ oz. heavy cream

2 bar spoons Monin chestnut syrup

---

1. Place all of the ingredients in a cocktail shaker, fill it two-thirds of the way with ice, and shake vigorously until chilled.

2. Double strain into the cocktail glass and enjoy.

BLUE CHEESE MARTINI

The ingredients make perfect sense if you think about it i
charcuterie terms: grapes, honey, and cheese.

1½ oz. Roquefort Cognac (see recipe)

½ oz. Sauternes

1 bar spoon agave nectar

---

1. Place all of the ingredients in a mixing glass and stir
   until combined.

2. Add ice to the mixing glass and stir until chilled.

3. Strain into the cocktail glass, garnish with the olive,
   and enjoy.

ROQUEFORT COGNAC: Place ¾ lb. Roquefort cheese in
a pan and melt it over medium heat. Transfer the melted cheese to a large mason jar, add 700 ml Hennessy VS
Cognac, and mix with an immersion blender. Transfer the
mixture to a flask and distill in a rotary evaporator at a
pressure of 30 mbar, with the hot bath at 100°F. Gradually
increase the rotation speed from 50 to 150 rpm. When yo
have extracted 500 ml, add 150 ml mineral water, bottle
infusion, and store at room temperature.

GLASSWARE: Coupe

GARNISH: Strip of lemon peel

THE JEROME

Verjus, the juice of unripe wine grapes, is becoming an increasingly common cocktail component, as it is capable of adding a sour element without also introducing acid to the equation.

1½ oz. Calvados VSOP

1 teaspoon Suze

½ oz. Pierre Ferrand Cognac

⅞ oz. verjus

2 dashes of orange bitters

2 teaspoons Rich Simple Syrup (see page 59)

2 dashes of Peychaud's bitters

1¾ oz. Roederer Estate Brut Champagne, to top

---

1. Place all of the ingredients, except for the Champagne, in a mixing glass, add a large ice cube, and stir until chilled.

2. Strain into the coupe and top with the Champagne.

3. Garnish with the strip of lemon peel and enjoy.

GLASSWARE: Rocks glass
GARNISH: Peach wedge

JOURNEY'S ESSENCE

The floral Hibiscus Pisco is buoyed by sweet and fruity elements, while the Muscat adds a little more body to the overall drink.

1½ oz. Hibiscus Pisco (see recipe)

¾ oz. Muscat

7/8 oz. unfiltered apple juice

2 teaspoons fresh lemon juice

2 teaspoons Simple Syrup (see page 26)

3 drops of peach essence

---

1. Place all of the ingredients in a cocktail shaker, fill it two-thirds of the way with ice, and shake vigorously until chilled.

2. Double strain over a large ice cube into the rocks glass, garnish with the peach wedge, and enjoy.

HIBISCUS PISCO: Place a 750 ml bottle of pisco and ½ oz. dried hibiscus blossoms in a mason jar and let steep for 1 hour. Strain before using or storing.

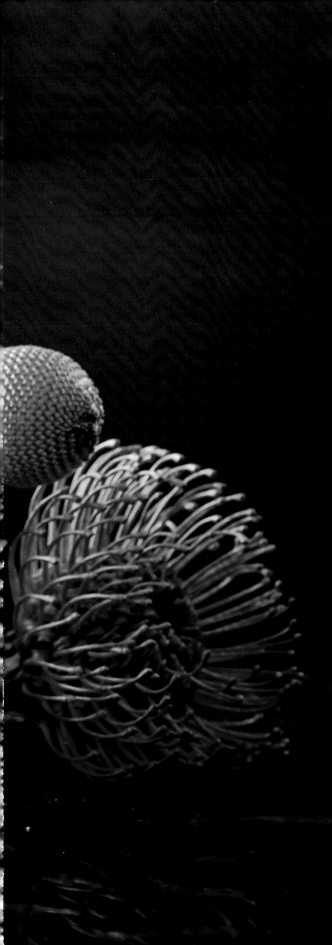

GLASSWARE: Large snifter

GARNISH: None

BAIJIU

An inspired take on the Bijou cocktail that was originally created by the father of modern bartending, Harry Johnson. It leads off with an intense burst of citrus that gives way to earthy and herbaceous notes.

⅞ oz. Suntory roku gin

1 oz. Carpano antica formula sweet vermouth

2 teaspoons Green Chartreuse

1 teaspoon Hong Kong baijiu

½ teaspoon Campari

2 drops of citric acid

3 dashes of orange bitters

---

1. Chill the snifter in the freezer.

2. Place all of the ingredients in a cocktail shaker, fill it two-thirds of the way with ice, and shake vigorously until chilled.

3. Double strain over a large ice cube into the chilled snifter and enjoy.

GLASSWARE: Coupe

GARNISH: Maraschino cherry

REVERSED MANHATTAN

A spicy, flipped Manhattan that just may become your new favorite come fall.

1⅓ oz. Chile-Infused Cinzano Rosso (see recipe)

⅔ oz. rye whiskey

Dash of Angostura bitters

---

1. Place all of the ingredients in a mixing glass, fill it two-thirds of the way with ice, and stir until chilled.

2. Strain into the cocktail glass, garnish with the maraschino cherry, and enjoy.

CHILE-INFUSED CINZANO ROSSO: Slice two small chile peppers lengthwise, place them in a skillet, and toast them for 3 to 4 minutes, turning them as necessary. Place the toasted chiles and 4 cups Cinzano Rosso sweet vermouth and steep for 2 hours. Strain before using or storing.

NEW-STYLE VERMOUTH COCKTAIL

Despite its name, this cocktail is keyed by the Luxardo, show-casing its ability to amplify and bring out the best in other ingredients.

---

1 whole lemon peel

2 oz. dry vermouth

2 bar spoons Luxardo maraschino liqueur

2 bar spoons Angostura bitters

1 bar spoon Simple Syrup (see page 26)

3 lemon slices

---

1. Place the lemon peel and vermouth in a mixing glass and muddle.

2. Add the remaining ingredients and ice to the mixing glass and stir until chilled.

3. Strain into the coupe and enjoy.

CHOCOLATE BURDOCK MARTINI

Burdock has been used in beverages for at least a millennium. The Europeans added it to gruit, an early bittering agen for beer. Brits ferment it with dandelion stems. Americans enjoy it in root beer. And here its delectable earthiness balances the sweetness of the chocolate and sherry.

2 oz. Burdock & Cacao Nib Brandy (see recipe)

½ oz. chocolate liqueur

2 bar spoons Pedro Ximénez sherry

1 bar spoon maple syrup

3 dashes of orange bitters

1. Place all of the ingredients in a cocktail shaker, fill it two-thirds of the way with ice, and shake vigorously until chilled.

2. Strain over a large ice cube into the coupe, garnish with the slice of burdock, and enjoy.

BURDOCK & CACAO NIB BRANDY: Place 1 stick of raw burdock, 1 tablespoon cacao nibs, and 700 ml of brandy in a large mason jar and steep for 3 days. Strain before using or bottling.

CUZCO MARTINI

By balancing the herbal and earthy notes of pisco with spicy jalapeño and the foresty flavor of rosemary, one can travel from the city to the country in a single sip.

---

1 slice of jalapeño chile pepper

½ oz. agave nectar

1 sprig of fresh rosemary

½ oz. fresh lemon juice

2 oz. pisco

---

1. Place the jalapeño and agave nectar in a cocktail shaker and muddle.

2. Add ice and the remaining ingredients and shake vigorously until chilled.

3. Strain into the cocktail glass, garnish with the truffle oil, and enjoy.

GLASSWARE: Rocks glass

GARNISH: Apple slices, cinnamon

LITTLE GREEN APPLES

This cocktail is sure to warm you in the depths of winter, but it can be turned to any time you're in the mood for a complex, bold drink, as the tart, sour notes of apple cider vinegar in the shrub are a natural balance to the sweetness of the brown sugar.

1 oz. Apple Cider Shrub (see recipe)

1½ oz. Cognac

½ oz. Zubrówka bison grass vodka

2 dashes of Angostura bitters

1. Place all of the ingredients in a mixing glass, fill it two-thirds of the way with ice, and stir until chilled.

2. Strain over a large ice cube into the rocks glass, garnish with apple slices and cinnamon, and enjoy.

APPLE CIDER SHRUB: Place 1⅓ cups brown sugar and 1⅓ cups water in a saucepan and bring to a boil, stirring to dissolve the sugar. Add 2 cups diced Royal Gala apples, reduce the heat, and simmer for 30 minutes. Add 1 cup apple cider vinegar, raise the heat, and return to a boil. Reduce the heat and simmer for 30 minutes. Remove the pan from heat and let the shrub cool completely. Strain through cheesecloth before using or storing.

METRIC CONVERSIONS

US Measurement	Approximate Metric Liquid Measurement	Approximate Metric Dry Measurement
1 teaspoon	5 ml	5 g
1 tablespoon or ½ ounce	15 ml	14 g
1 ounce or ⅛ cup	30 ml	29 g
¼ cup or 2 ounces	60 ml	57 g
⅓ cup	80 ml	76 g
½ cup or 4 ounces	120 ml	113 g
⅔ cup	160 ml	151 g
¾ cup or 6 ounces	180 ml	170 g
1 cup or 8 ounces or ½ pint	240 ml	227 g
1½ cups or 12 ounces	350 ml	340 g
2 cups or 1 pint or 16 ounces	475 ml	454 g
3 cups or 1½ pints	700 ml	680 g
4 cups or 2 pints or 1 quart	950 ml	908 g

ABOUT CIDER MILL PRESS
BOOK PUBLISHERS

Good ideas ripen with time. From seed to harvest, Cider Mill Press brings fine reading, information, and entertainment together between the covers of its creatively crafted books. Our Cider Mill bears fruit twice a year, publishing a new crop of titles each spring and fall.

"Where Good Books Are Ready for Press"

501 Nelson Place
Nashville, Tennessee 37214

cidermillpress.com